THE SOPHISTS

THE SOPHISTS

Rhetoric, Democracy, and Plato's Idea of Sophistry

HAROLD BARRETT
California State University, Hayward

Chandler & Sharp Publishers, Inc.
Novato, California

Notices of Copyright and Literary Property appear on page 82.

Library of Congress Cataloging in Publication Data

Barrett, Harold
    The sophists : rhetoric, democracy, and Plato's
idea of sophistry.

    Bibliography: pp. 77–81.
    Includes index.
    1. Sophists (Greek philosophy)   2. Rhetoric   3. Plato
I. Title.
B288.B37 1987   183′.1   87-21051
ISBN 0–88316–557–0

Book designed by Jon Sharp.
Cover design and art by Jacki Gallagher.
Edited by W. L. Parker.
Composition by Publications Services of Marin.

Contents

Contents

Preface

This little book is offered in the spirit of the sophists: for both general reader and serious student, as an aid to furthering understanding on a topic of relevance to our times. It is intended as a *useful* statement, to all who would be reminded of our common Greek heritage and who wish to increase their appreciation of the important role played by those sometimes praised and sometimes maligned great teachers of the fifth century before the Christian era.

A number of scholars in their writings have contributed to the establishment of the sophists as significant figures in the history of western thought, for instance, Grote, Hegel, and Mill of the nineteenth century and more recently Eric A. Havelock, Everett Lee Hunt, G. B. Kerferd, Mario Untersteiner, and others. One who comes after these estimable authors finds them a grand "support group" who provide not only knowledge and strong argument but also firm ground for confidence in one's own conclusions about the sophists. Making no claim on adding to their scholarship, this book seeks mainly to raise up for proper acknowledgment the place of early Greek sophists in the history of rhetoric and to set their work apart from Plato's famous polemic in building his idea of sophistry. An attendant aim is to confirm the necessary connection of rhetorical usage to democratic process. To realize these goals, it is essential to meet Plato and utilize his valuable evidence on things said and done, while remaining respectfully aware of his manifest objectives and philosophical predispositions.

Kerferd observes in *The Sophistic Movement* that "in the modern world where the majority of scholars are not Platonists . . . it is something of a paradox that the Platonic condemnation still remains largely unquestioned." But we do question, if for no other reason than that the idea of rhetoric — the sophists' principal subject — is terribly consequential and too precious for us to permit ascendancy of the Platonic idea of sophistry. With the sophists' efforts, rhetoric became one of the first disciplines and was advanced as an idea of value and permanence. After the sophists, we have come to know that conduct of a good life and realization of social good may depend as much on awareness of rhetorical principles as on lessons of Plato's great dialogues.

Yet the sophists require no more from us than recognition of their teaching as indispensable and worthy. It answered human need, even while challenged — and so it will always be with beneficial but threatening innovation.

I wish to add a personal note of gratitude to Professors Bower Aly, Carroll Arnold, John E. Baird, Harry Caplan, Frank D. Gilliard, Everett Lee Hunt, James J. Murphy, and Joe Sue for information and inspiration. I am pleased to recall that it was Dr. Aly in his course in classical rhetoric who introduced me to Dean Hunt's "Plato and Aristotle on Rhetoric and Rhetoricians," an essay that many of us consider basic to an understanding of philosophical distinctions among Plato, Aristotle, and the sophists. That event marked the start of my opening a place for the sophists — alongside Isocrates, Aristotle, and others who figure prominently in the history of rhetoric in Greece. Then came supportive words of Professor Caplan on visiting Greece and working at the American School of Classical Studies: to enjoy the plenteous resources of the Blegen Library and association of scholars in the classics — and from there to explore the museums, historical sites, and all that Greece continues to offer students of the past.

A particular acknowledgment is due Willis L. Parker, editor. The book is better for his keen eye, sound judgment, and admirable professional care.

Thanks to Lorraine Zeyen, my expert and accommodating typist of many manuscripts of the past twenty years.

Also, I wish to acknowledge the library and librarians of my university: partners in scholarship.

I am grateful to Jonathan Sharp for his faith in the book, publisher's good sense, and aesthetic judgment.

And now I have a request: that Carol who gave support at all steps along the way — in London, in Athens and Papagos, and in California — accept an equal share of satisfaction in the result.

THE SOPHISTS

To the Memory of Professors
Bower Aly, Harry Caplan, and
Everett Lee Hunt: Friends and Mentors

1
SOPHIST

*T*he name "sophist" appeared in discourse of the Greek people as early as in the sixth century,* in reference to poets, musicians, wise men, philosophers, or other accomplished and admired persons. Though often applied respectfully, it could be used to deride or criticize, as writings of the early fifth century reveal. For example, in *Prometheus Bound*, Aeschylus has Hermes put down Prometheus, the great benefactor of mankind, by naming him "You, the sophist, who have sinned against the gods." When suspicious of another's intelligence or visible learning, of someone in a teaching role for example, ancient Greeks occasionally turned to the word "sophist," much as people today find disparaging use for "intellectual" (Guthrie 27-34) or "egghead."

Later, "sophist" came to designate professional teacher. It is this usage and members of this group that are the subject here. Standing out among the sophists of the fifth century are Protagoras, Gorgias, Prodicus, Hippias, and Thrasymachus: five noteworthy representatives of the "older sophists," the first professional teachers and important contributors to the history of rhetorical theory and

---

*This is the sixth century before the birth of Jesus. Nearly all dates in this book refer to times or periods that preceded the Christian era, principally the fifth century when the five sophists flourished and the following century—the fourth—which was Plato's day.

practice. My purpose is to acknowledge the product of their efforts, while distinguishing it from Plato's rhetorical representation of sophists and his idea of sophistry.

FOREIGNERS IN ATHENS

All five were traveling teachers, and it is important to remember that none was a citizen of Athens. Protagoras was from Abdera in the northeast of Greece; Gorgias was from the Sicilian town of Leontini; Prodicus's home was the island of Ceos; Hippias came from Elis and Thrasymachus from faraway Chalcedon. In Athens, these people were *metics*, resident aliens with limited rights. For example, they could not marry an Athenian woman or own land, except through a special grant. Though metics enjoyed certain privileges and legal protection, they were not allowed to participate directly in the city's political life. Generally, it may be said that foreigners in Athens were accepted for contributions that they made to commerce, industry, and the arts, yet their position was less secure and advantageous than a citizen's.

To advertise their offerings, the sophists used a sample lecture — an *epideixis* — as an oral public announcement before gatherings in the Agora and other public places. They held their classes in private dwellings or various public places such as school buildings or grounds, where many Athenians welcomed their teaching and paid them well for it. But by accepting money for their services and claiming success in teaching, the sophists came into conflict with rival educators and other Athenians.

THEIR CURRICULUM AND CLIENTELE

All of the prominent fifth-century sophists taught rhetoric in some form. Moreover, instruction in this art was the fundamental common emphasis. But viewed collectively, the sophists taught a number of other subjects, including grammar, literature, mathematics, astronomy, geography, and history. They offered short courses, long courses, and single lectures. All were well educated. Most were polymaths — persons of great breadth in learning — and versatile teachers, though individuals had their special interests. Flourishing during a time of great expansion of knowledge — and contributing to it — the sophists presented a varied and wide curriculum.

Too, theirs was a practical curriculum, designed to teach the Greek ideal of *aretê*: the knowledge and attitude for effective participation in domestic, social, and political life. Their courses were valuable to a young man who would take a place in managing civic affairs and assume a position of prestige in the community. Speaking ability was essential for him. Without competence in enforcing an argument, a man's power in the legislative assembly or law courts was limited. Young Greeks were eager for the sophists' instruction in civic goodness, in the wisdom and skill that were basic to serving the city and gaining prominence. Given conditions of the time, it is no wonder that lessons of the sophists were attractive. In our terms, the sophists were progressive and innovative leaders in an educational reform characterized by highly functional instruction.

Their immediate clientele were not the masses certainly, but people with leisure and sufficient money to pay the fees. Given the excitement that a sophist's appearance generated and the hungering among the citizenry for intellectual and cultural nourishment, one can imagine the disappointment of those left out. Their participation had to be indirect. Yet it cannot be said that they were not affected by the sophists' teaching. Everyone was, sooner or later. As students of the sophists became people of influence, results of their education were felt in the city and abroad. Too, the sophists' presence in the city went beyond teaching. They attended social gatherings, recited and declaimed at important festivals, engaged with general audiences in spontaneous question-and-answer encounters, lectured publicly upon occasion, gave funeral orations, and published their ideas in written form.

Tempting though it is, one cannot speak of the sophists as developers of a single "program" or as participants in a cohesive "movement," for theirs were not coordinated or unified efforts in any sense. Their activities did not tend collectively toward some definite end, except as we view them in retrospect. Looking back, we do discern patterns and make connections among persons and their respective theories, but we must remember that the sophists operated as individuals — and in competition with one another. Nonetheless, taken together, their courses might be thought of as a full curriculum in higher education and as a body of subject matter to prepare a man for leadership in the city.

MEETING A NEED

The fifth century saw rapid growth of democracy in Greece. After the liberalization of political and social structures of Athens by the famous statesman Solon early in the sixth century there came the sweeping reforms of Cleisthenes late in that century. Cleisthenes, an archon in Athens — or leading magistrate — was the author of far-reaching provisions on self-government and voting privileges. He is sometimes named as the father of Athenian democracy. Then followed new and more popular legislation and active application of democratic procedures by the statesmen Ephialtes and Pericles in the fifth century. In the sophists' time, political power was transferred from the Areopagus to the Assembly: from the elite to the many. For democrats, the new conditions were exciting and promising. Yet to assume the responsibilities thrust upon them and to take advantage of opportunities made available, people had to equip themselves with knowledge and specific skills, lest political control and legal rights be theirs in name only. The uses of democracy are not enjoyed by the ignorant or unsophisticated. The Athenians' need was for general learning, civic awareness, and capability in discerning issues, shaping and enforcing arguments, and responding to opposing arguments with effect. The sophists offered the necessary lessons.

Other great changes came about in the fifth century. It was a time of expanded scientific knowledge and burgeoning intellectual inquiry and questioning, of debate on topics of moral and social significance that had never been posed before. The sophists represented the antithesis to major schools of thought in their day. Indeed, they came as a presumptuous and contrasting wave behind the heavy swell of the Ionian theorists of the sixth century and the kind of intellectualism that seeks knowledge for its own sake. As speculative thinkers, the Ionians in the east (from an area that is part of present-day Turkey) had developed new and compelling theories in science and philosophy which spread across Greece and held sway until met by the sophists' ideas on human behavior and potential. It was the sophists who turned intellectual attention from abstract Ionian speculation and concentration on the natural world to more immediate problems of people and religion, people and law, people and the state, and the like. They were *humanists,* not in the sense of secular humanism as criticized today, but as persons who believed in humankind's capability of improving itself and in being responsible for its choices. The sophists followed a principle of *subjectivity,* which affirmed "that it is the thinking and perceiving subject himself who determines his own thoughts and perceptions," not forces in nature (Kerferd *Sophistic Movement* 7). The sophists directed the community to social and legal issues, ethics, and concerns of the individual person. They demonstrated significance in questions bearing on the effective functioning of people in a dynamic and — in their eyes — competitive society.

Also, the sophists found Greeks of the fifth century to be deficient in what we might call "rhetorical appreciation," a lack of social awareness that may be attributed in part to the power of Ionian detachment from social concern. Uses of rhetoric are rejected if the dominant view is that discovery of the true and real is sufficient unto itself: that an intervening agency is not required to make it known and effective. Operating too was a basic fear of democracy, a mistrust of people's capacity to govern themselves fairly and well. Appreciation of rhetoric derived from a realistic perception that persuasion was useful and necessary to citizens of a democratic and culturally blooming city, for example, in advocacy and counter-advocacy in the law courts and the political arena. Appreciation of rhetoric was needed to answer the naivete behind the opinion that persuasion exemplified a deceitful side of human behavior. In a word, the sophists sought to teach people of the fifth century a lesson in maturity: to accept themselves as social creatures striving together in an active, changing society, but with individual pursuits and rich opportunities available through practical education.

2

FIVE SOPHISTS OF THE FIFTH CENTURY

*W*ho were those teachers of the fifth century? What specifically did they believe and do? How were they like one another? How were they different? The following are brief biographical sketches of five outstanding figures. Accounts of Protagoras and Gorgias, the earliest professional sophists and the most prominent, will be first and most extensive.

PROTAGORAS

Protagoras was from Abdera, a city three or four hundred miles northeast of Athens. His dates are impossible to establish, but he probably was born around 485, perhaps earlier. He lived for sixty or seventy years and was a contemporary of such illustrious people as Pericles, matchless leader and orator; playwrights Sophocles and Euripides, and the historian Herodotus.

Quite probably, Protagoras was the first teacher to charge pupils a fee: the equivalent of several thousand dollars for a typical course of study. Among the subjects taught by Protagoras during his forty-year career are argumentation and debate, ethics, jurisprudence, grammar and diction, oratory, and politics. Though but two or three fragments of his works survive, he wrote a number of books and on diverse subjects: politics, mathematics, law, ethics, human behavior, correct speaking, religion, philosophy, and others. Protagoras believed that virtue could be taught, that men could improve their condition through education, and that competent, educated men deserved society's respect and rewards. In the dialogue of Plato bearing his name, Protagoras stated that his instruction "consists in bringing about a right perception and understanding of the best way of regulating one's own family affairs, and similarly as regards citizenship, in qualifying men both to speak on the affairs of the state, and to do the best for the state."

Though known principally as a teacher, Protagoras had other involvements. One of them was as formulator of a code of laws. The assignment followed one of his visits to Athens and his meeting Pericles. The two became friends and once spent an entire day discussing — and perhaps debating — legal issues relevant to the case of a man who was killed by an athlete's javelin. Was the athlete responsible for the tragedy? The victim? The javelin itself? Pericles and Protagoras came to enjoy mutual respect and when Athens had the opportunity to establish the new colony at Thurii in southern Italy, it was Protagoras whom Athens's leading political figure sent there to write the laws. Pericles's choice of Protagoras for this important assignment is obvious testimony to the sophist's competence in jurisprudence, not to mention his political and rhetorical ability.

To students of rhetoric, Protagoras's most exciting belief is that on every argument there are two sides, one opposing the other (see Diogenes Laertius, IX). That Protagoras was apparently the first person to make this assertion and teach rhetoric accordingly indicates how a study of his life and times can take one back to the very beginnings of certain vital ideas, which we today assume to have been "truths" of all times. Imbedded in the statement are several precepts upon which modern systems of justice and democratic disputation rest. All questions are controversial, suggested Protagoras. The "truth" of one side will be tested by the "truth" of the other. Advocates of both sides have the burden of proving their sides the stronger. Feeble representation by one side or the other amounts to neglect of responsibility. Protagoras's dictum is accepted today as the core of the adversary system of justice, legislative deliberations, and academic debate. But in Protagoras's time this novel notion was alarming to many, especially those who believed that known truths are undebatable. To them, instruction which put pupils to questioning TRUTHS and upholding the "other side," bent them toward making "the worse appear the better." Incidentally, this judgment eventually became an indictment of all sophists. But to Protagoras it was important that his pupils understand both sides, for right choices cannot be reached without examination of opposing arguments. To implement his principle, he had his pupils explore issues that he put before them and debate propositions pro and con.

Perhaps the most threatening of Protagoras's beliefs is that "man is the measure of all things," one fragment of his writings that has been preserved. But what did Protagoras mean? It is a strong statement and certainly suggests Protagoras's relativism, which Gregory Vlastos emphasizes in his modern dialogue on the subject (xii–xvi):

— [When you say "man is the measure of all things"], What "man" are you talking about?

Protagoras. Every man, you, me, anybody.

— Even men who haven't studied science or philosophy?

Prot. Aren't they men?

— But these men go by appearances; they haven't the sense to distinguish appearance from reality.

Prot. And they are perfectly right. Appearance *is* reality. Even what philosophers call "reality" is just what appears true to them.

— But appearances are not consistent. The same wind often feels warm to me, cold to you.

Prot. Then it *is* warm for you, cold for me.

— But what is it in itself?

Prot. "Wind-in-itself"? I know of no such thing. Do you? The only wind you can know is the one you can feel: this is the wind-for-you, and you are its measure.

— If that is the way you reason, you might as well hold that all beliefs are true.

Prot. I do. All beliefs *are* true for those who believe them.

— But that is fantastic.

Prot. I can prove that no such thing as a false belief can exist. Suppose it did, it would have to be about something or about nothing. It couldn't be about nothing: you can't even think of nothing. So it must be about something — something real for you, else why should you be thinking about it? And if your belief is about something real for you, how can it be false for you?

— Nonsense. There are millions of false beliefs.

Prot. Mention one that is false for him who believes it.

— Will you accept an example from geometry?

Prot. Gladly.

— Tell the man in the street that a tangent touches a circle at just one point, and he'll swear you are wrong. Would you say his belief is true?

Prot. True for him. The only tangent for him is the one he can see; and you are not going to tell me that he can *see* a tangent that touches a circle at just one point.

— I suppose you have no scruples about applying your appearance-is-reality doctrine to morals.

Prot. Are you insinuating there is something unscrupulous about that? I am in most respectable company here. Herodotus, you will recall, said Cambyses was mad because he despised the burial customs of other people. All I am doing is to generalize the notion our historian has applied to something as sacrosanct as funeral rites, and say that anything held right and just in a given state is right and just for it.

Protagoras's view that "man is the measure of all things" was as controversial as his believing that premises are debatable, and critics condemned it — and its author — as placing the judgment of mere men over the gods' authority. Yet his pedagogy in debate is consistent with it. Protagoras probably meant that individuals, each using a unique mind and set of senses, necessarily see things differently, develop different perspectives, and come to differing conclusions. All the more reason for examination and testing of both sides of a question. One person's truth may not be another's. Good proposals are those that survive rigorous debate. Protagoras advanced a practical epistemology, a functional way of knowing.

A topic addressed in one way or another by all five sophists and their contemporaries was the relative influence of law and nature on human conduct. Protagoras's position is liberal, we would say. Believing in human betterment, he followed the "law side," against the contention that people were restricted by their "nature." Laws and customs are derived from social agreement, not from human nature, he held; and they are good insofar as they help people function together in society. He believed that a person was not bound by nature and could create change. People could improve their lot and social conditions, acquire an education, rise in the social order. Needless to say, the price was responsibility for their own behavior.

This position countered the view that found social conditions and levels as "naturally" determined and fixed. Protagoras viewed society as moving and open, not static and closed. From his perspective, learning and convention dominated in affecting the ways people came to their codes of ethics, political structures, and social perspectives. Thus an aristocrat was not *naturally* a gentleman (nor a peasant *naturally* ungentlemanly). A person developed through learning and what we might call culturation. It is not surprising that this radical doctrine threatened people at high social levels who felt that their gentility and strength had been inherited, felt that *by nature* they were better and *naturally* aristocratic. The belief in convention and law as more powerful than nature connects directly to belief in equality among people, that all are equal before the law.

To understand the force of fifth-century Athenian criticism of Protagoras, consider his writing on religion, of which we have this fragment:

> Concerning the gods, I am not able to know to a certainty whether they exist or whether they do not. For there are many things which prevent one from knowing, especially the obscurity of the subject, and the shortness of the life of man.

Is this agnosticism or honest skepticism? Diogenes Laertius wrote that this frank admission led to the public burning of all books written by Protagoras as well as his banishment from Athens. The story is not accepted by many historians, but whether accurate or not, it does bear witness to the power of Protagoras's ideas. Such was the imaginable fate of one who held that individuals' knowledge, religion, and truth are colored by their perceptions, limitations, and external conditions.

GORGIAS

Gorgias's native city was the Greek colony of Leontini in Sicily, several hundred miles across the sea from Athens. Born in the 490s or 480s, he lived for more than 100 years. His important position in the chain of influential figures who were noteworthy in the history of rhetorical theory and practice is apparent if one observes that the Sicilian rhetorician Corax taught Tisias, who may have taught Gorgias, who taught Isocrates. From there one can connect to Cicero and even to Winston Churchill (Hadas xvi). The Tisias-Gorgias link is the weakest in the chain, but we do know that they were associates. Tisias may have accompanied Gorgias on his famous Sicilian embassy to Athens in 427. It was a political trip but more remembered by us for its rhetorical consequences, as the beginning point of Gorgias's phenomenal career in Athens.

Diodorus Siculus, historian of the first century before the Christian era, tells of his visit:

> At this time in Sicily the people of Leontini, who were colonists of the Chalcideans but relatives of the Athenians, happened to be involved in war with the Syracusans. Being hard pressed in the war and in danger of being forcibly overrun because of the numerical superiority of the Syracusans, they sent ambassadors to Athens, asking the democracy to come to their aid as quickly as possible and to rescue their city from its dangers. . . . The chief of the delegation was the orator Gorgias, in power of speech by far the most eminent of the men of his time. (Kennedy trans. 32)

Subsequently, Gorgias either lived in Athens or visited there frequently. Gorgias had many opportunities to address Athenian audiences, and he charmed them from the start. Both amazed and instructed by his extraordinary, dazzling oratory, particularly his verbal innovations, they received him enthusiastically. Particularly captivating were his poetic rhythms, choices and patterns of words that fell like lyrics, unconventional figures of speech, and so forth. Philostratus, writer on lives of the sophists, presents Gorgias as

> an example of forcefulness and of unexpected expression and of inspiration and of the grand style for great subjects and of detached phrases and transitions, by which speech becomes sweeter than it has been and more impressive. . . . he also introduced poetic words for ornament and dignity. . . . he . . . improvised easily, and it is no wonder if he was admired by many when he spoke in Athens, although by then an old man. . . . (Kennedy trans, 31–32)

Gorgias's usages formed a style which very likely had never been heard before by Athenian audiences. His was a new oratory, as much poetical as rhetorical. Moreover, he was a ready speaker, doubtless a master in the preparation and use of commonplaces, with ability to speak on many subjects. He was skilled in refutation of opponents' arguments, advising, as Aristotle reports approvingly in the *Rhetoric*, that "the opposition's seriousness is to be demolished by laughter, and the laughter by seriousness."

"Speech is a powerful lord," Gorgias declared in his encomium of Helen, "which by means of the finest and most invisible body effects the divinest works: it can stop fear and banish grief and create joy and nurture piety."

Buoyed by glorious initial success, Gorgias traveled to other cities as well, teaching rhetoric, demonstrating his art, and giving speeches on special occasions, for example to the throngs attending the great ceremonies at the Olympic and Pythian Games. The speeches he read at those festivals are not extant, but we do have his "Encomium of Helen" and "Defense on Behalf of Palamedes" — neither of which was written for a single, specific occasion — and a fragment of his "Funeral Oration."

Gorgias's scope in teaching was narrower than Protagoras's for he centered on oratory, mainly epideictic — for special occasions such as festivals — though not ignoring forensic art. Unlike Protagoras, he did not claim to teach *aretê*, though doubtless he did, at least indirectly, as every experienced teacher might surmise. In the course of his teaching and speaking, Gorgias developed a wide following and exerted much influence on rhetorical activity of his day.

Gorgias used his own compositions as models for pupils to study, and analysis of his "Helen" yields an understanding of essential elements in his theory and emphases in teaching, particularly on organization, selection and development of thought, and style. His subject is the wife of Menelaus and most beautiful of all Greek women, whose abduction by Paris led to the Trojan War, according to Homer's story. Brief and compact, the speech doubtless includes usages of rhetoric that Gorgias wished to stress with his pupils. It is an artistic piece — something of a rhetorical exercise or demonstration — showing what can be done with available technique. A partial text is included as Appendix B.

The encomium — a speech of praise — offers samples of the kind of oratory with which Gorgias delighted the people of Athens. In explication, we see that his opening statement — his proem — is brief but perhaps not disproportionately so. His clear statement of purpose — "to free the accused of blame" and from the ignorance of those who accuse her — is matched by organization of thought which has textbook excellence. After comment on Helen's background, he unfolds four causal arguments one by one, as distinct main heads of a neat analysis. Helen's leaving Greece for Troy with the young prince was occasioned by one of four forces: love, persuasion, force, or divine intervention. Apparent too are transitional aids to provide cohesion. In the epilogue — the concluding remarks — Gorgias reiterates his final judgment: "not to blame Helen." Then he summarizes his main points and makes an aside reference to another reason for writing the speech — personal diversion. Quite obviously, Gorgias recognized the importance of clarity in purpose and organization, with the aid of his own speeches as models, and he instructed his pupils accordingly.

As George Kennedy relates (168–170), Gorgias built his argument with the *apagogic* method which involved naming various alternatives or reasons, then examining them, one at a time. Gorgias cited the four possible causes for Helen's leaving and weighed them against each other, in a "this-opposing-that" and "but-on-the-other-hand" system of argumentation. The apagogic is a juxtaposing of conflicting premises, allowing a kind of dialectical clash, and, as practiced by Gorgias, giving the audience a feeling for the dissonance in argument that he created. The result was a vivid contrasting of good and bad, right and wrong, strong and weak, etc. Thus, his appeal in "Helen" was at once reasonable and lively.

Clearly, Gorgias's argumentation is didactic, obvious and academic. Rhetoric as a formal art was young in Gorgias's day. And in his "Helen," he wanted to demonstrate available rhetorical wares and to be letter perfect in practice. One cannot know to what extent his more "public" speeches, for example those given at Olympia and Delphi, were as pedantic as his "Helen" (and "Palamedes"). It does seem likely, however, that in all of them he pleased with a winsome and novel style.

Elements of pathos (emotional appeal), intermixed with logos (use of reason), accounted for much of the power of his "Helen," an observation that will be more evident in discussion of style later on. But continuing an analysis of his apagogic mode of proving, we see that in Gorgias's use it was clearly a stimulator of listener involvement and response. It insisted on a battle among ideas, on an agonistic clash promoting excitement. Thus in "Helen," Gorgias structured an "adversary" relation among ideas in testing arguments. In this sense, Gorgias and Protagoras had a common base in theory. Recall the latter's dictum on every argument having two sides. Through form, Gorgias built in agitation and competition of reasons; form contributed to substance.

One can conceive of development of ethos — personal proof — through the apagogic mode of argumentation as handled by the artist Gorgias. His *balancing* of words and phrases — his careful weighing of this and that — bespeak *fairness* in analysis and *equality* in treatment of issues. Gorgias gave an *exposition* of causes and in appearance did not engage in direct *persuasion*. Appearing innocent of bias in setting forth his reasoning fully and justly, he demonstrated credibility.

Such, then, are uses of an apagogic method, of which the sophisticated Gorgias must have been aware as he prepared the encomium of Helen and referred it as a model to his students.

An understanding of features in his style helps explain Gorgian rhetorical magic in delighting and holding an audience, for elements of language were inseparable from the fundamental structure of his reasoning. Neither can be reviewed in isolation. As a pioneer, free of the tyranny of rhetorical canon, Gorgias found poetical modes to be useful in oratory. His "Helen" is a profusion of rhyme and meter, repetitive patterns, forms of verbal contrasts, and figures of speech. Parallel construction, particularly antithesis, was basic to his use of the apagogic (evidencing the necessary unity of thought and style) and served to catch the audience up in the back-and-forth movement of argument. If many of the usages and words seem forced and "unnatural" to us, or inappropriate, perhaps it is because we are unable to understand the appeal of this kind of ornamentation to audiences in the fifth century. Its very novelty enhanced its attractiveness, as noted in the visual and graphic quality in his discourse. Style is a large contributor to this effect. One can *picture* his ideas and distinguish sharply among them. Moreover, projection of thought was immeasurably intensified in actual delivery, with employment of the many vocal strategies at the command of a brilliant Greek speaker of the fifth century.

Gorgias's conception of *kairos* relates to his choices in idea, organization, and style. Central to his rhetorical theory and practice, *kairos* is a doctrine on adaptation, specifically to demands of audience and occasion. Speakers were to be aware of the *kairos* of a rhetorical situation and to respond appropriately. Thus Gorgias's selection of material, structuring, elements of style, timing, and the like, were dictated by *kairos*.

Gorgias the sophist was a prominent and highly influential rhetorical figure, affecting the careers of many, including another famous teacher, Isocrates, the historian Thucydides, and the physician Hippocrates. He drew Athens to his feet when he arrived there in 427, producing what Professor W. R. M. Lamb called a "sudden bout of Gorgiasm" (150). Sudden, yes — and sustained.

PRODICUS

Prodicus's home was Ceos, an island lying off the coast of Athens. He was born between 470 and 460 and lived for some years after the death of Socrates in 399. Not much biographical information on Prodicus is available, but we do know that he visited Athens frequently as ambassador to that city. While there, he engaged in public speaking and declaimed his compositions, for which he became well known and respected. Finding that Athenians — and people of other cities — had a keen interest in higher education, Prodicus offered his services as teacher.

Like all sophists, he responded to demand and emphasized rhetoric in his teaching. Apparently his courses were less varied than most other sophists', but he did include logic, ethics, and related subjects. Socrates not only took instruction from him but confessed that he would send to Prodicus those young men who were unable to profit from his — Socrates's — instruction. Others who probably were taught by Prodicus are Euripides, the teacher Isocrates, and the sophist Thrasymachus. Prodicus is the author of *On Nature* and *On the Nature of Man*.

Extant is Prodicus's parable, "Choice of Heracles," an *epideixis* or set piece illustrating one method of his teaching. Constructed to teach a lesson on morality, the story is of young Heracles (the hero Hercules) who, when faced with the decision on what road to travel in life, meets two female figures, one named Vice and the other Virtue. The former, seductive in behavior and "wearing a costume such as made her physical ripeness easy to estimate," barged forward and asked Heracles to follow her in life. She promised no "wars or woes," no physical or mental struggle, and full satisfaction of all needs. Virtue, in her turn, is allowed the longest speeches. She will grant achievement of "honorable and wondrous deeds" but only if the "face of reality" is recognized: the gods benefit only those who struggle and persevere, are loyal, serve, lead the simple life, are disciplined, and practice other merits. When Vice interrupts, Virtue responds with a stirring and extremely idealistic rebuttal, contrasting her noble but rigorous course with that "Hussy's" moral deficiency and package of evils. The choice is Heracles's. A rendition is included as the Appendix C.

Prodicus was dedicated to promotion of precision in use of language, perhaps his chief contribution as sophist. He was an etymologist and semanticist who stressed right use of words, particularly distinctions among synonyms. He held that neglect in observing subtle meanings led to distortion of thought and from that to faulty communication. He attempted, said Aristotle in the *Topics,* "to assign to every term its own peculiar significance." For example, he distinguished three forms of pleasure: "joy," "delight," and "good cheer."

A zealot on right word usage, Prodicus reportedly made it his business to listen for errors and to check people whenever he heard them err. He became so well known for his single-minded interest in fostering vigilance in use of language that some people began to make jokes about it. In the *Cratylus,* Plato told of a discussion on proper use of names held by Socrates and two others. At one point, Socrates acknowledged that poverty had forced him to take the great Prodicus's single-drachma course instead of the one for fifty drachmas — therefore, he did not "know the truth about such matters" as knowledge of names. Though obviously a bit of mockery, and possibly deserved, Socrates's comment does point up Prodicus's reputation as a specialist in language.

In the *Protagoras,* Plato recounted how Prodicus, in the company of Socrates, Protagoras, Hippias, and others, made semantic distinctions in reference to proper listening, argumentation, and related topics.

> That, Critias, seems to me to be well said, for those who are present at such [controversial] discussions ought to be impartial hearers of both the speakers; remembering, however, that impartiality is not the same as equality, for both sides should be impartially heard, and yet an equal meed [regard] should not be assigned to both of them; but to the wiser a higher meed should be given, and a lower to the less wise. And I as well as Critias would beg you, Protagoras and Socrates, to grant our request, which is, that you will argue with one another and not wrangle; for friends argue with friends out of goodwill, but only adversaries and enemies wrangle. And then our meeting will be delightful; for in this way you, who are the speakers, will be most likely to win esteem, and not praise only, among us who are your audience; for esteem is a sincere conviction of the hearers' souls, but praise is often an insincere expression of men uttering falsehoods contrary to their conviction. And thus we who are the hearers will be gratified and not pleased; for gratification is of the mind when receiving wisdom and knowledge, but pleasure is of the body when eating or experiencing some other bodily delight.

Popular in the community, Prodicus sought to teach that language is not something sent from the heavens or from nature; it is a product of human agreement. He was a sensitizer on standards in language use who influenced both his contemporaries and later writers, not to mention the Attic Orators. Thus a significant area of rhetorical study got attention which might have been neglected but for the insistence of Prodicus.

HIPPIAS

Hippias was from Elis, a city in the Peloponnesus, not far from Olympia but well over 100 miles from Athens. He lived a long life and was active in 399, the year of Socrates's death. One might put his birthdate at any point between 485 and 445. Variations in estimations of Hippias's dates seem irreconcilable. Like Prodicus, he was relied upon often by his city for representation abroad. Prominent throughout Greece for his lectures and teaching, he became a wealthy man.

Hippias was a fascinating individual and led an unusually interesting life. His widowed daughter married Isocrates, who was then an old man. Hippias was widely read and was known as one of the most cosmopolitan men of his day. Studying the experiences and lives of many peoples — not only Greek — he found kinship among persons of all ethnic and cultural backgrounds.

Hippias delighted in recounting that when he spoke at the festival of Olympia all items adorning his body were his own creations. For that occasion, he made all the clothes he wore, including tunic, shoes, cloak, and girdle. Further, he made all other items on his person: ring, seal, oil flask, and body scraper for use on the skin after exercise.

At Olympia, besides presenting a prepared composition, he undertook to answer on the spot all questions put to him, regardless of subject.

Xenophon reported another instance of Hippias's self-assertiveness, this one involving Socrates. Arriving in Athens after a long absence, Hippias found Socrates discoursing with some friends on how remarkable it is that if a person wants someone taught shoe-making or carpentry or metal-work or horsemanship, it is easy to decide where to send him. Teachers are available. But where should someone be sent to learn justice? Hippias overheard the conversation and decided to have some fun.

"Are you still saying the same old things, Socrates, that I heard you saying long ago?"

Socrates replied, "Not only do I go on saying the same things, Hippias, but — stranger still — I say them on the same subjects. You, I daresay, with your wide learning, never say the same things on the same subjects."

Hippias responded with certainty, affirming that he always tried to have a new thought to say.

Socrates then asked if Hippias talked on things he knew, such as commonplace knowledge. He also wanted to know if Hippias at first said one thing but later said another. "Or on numbers, should someone ask you if twice five are ten, would you not give the same answer now as you did before?"

"On those matters, Socrates," said Hippias, "like yourself, I always say the same things. But on justice I am absolutely certain that I now have something to say that neither you nor anyone else could dispute."

These and other examples of swagger may testify to this sophist's conceit, which Hippias now and again did exhibit to fifth century Greeks, but truly, he was extraordinarily accomplished — the epitome of the polymath, versed in and prepared to teach an astounding array of subjects: history, music, phonetics, linguistics and grammar, astronomy, poetry and other forms of literature, politics, family genealogy, and mathematics — including arithmetic and geometry. An acknowledged scholar in geometry, Hippias is credited with at least one major discovery in that field: the curve called quadratrix. Moreover, he was conversant in theories of art and skilled in handicrafts.

Of special significance in the history of rhetoric is Hippias's fabulous memory, which enhanced his rhetorical powers and allowed him to impress people. For example, he could remember fifty names on one hearing — and in the order given. He developed techniques in memorizing and put the study of mnemonics into his curriculum, to teach others his way of retaining information.

Hippias's position in the law vs. nature controversy differed from other sophists'. He saw law as tyrannical and as forcing men to be in conflict with nature. But nature had universal laws, he held, which eventually reconciled conflicts and made social functioning possible.

Though none of Hippias's writings has survived, he was the author of epics, tragedies, verse, and other pieces. Some works thought to be his are a *Trojan Dialogue,* an *Elegy,* and a *List of Olympian Victors.*

THRASYMACHUS

Thrasymachus was born in Chalcedon, a city in Asia Minor near the legendary Troy. Though his dates are not available, we can assume that his most productive years were the three decades from about 430 to 400.

Thrasymachus was well known as an accomplished orator. Dionysius of Halicarnassus, critic and historian of the first century before the Christian era, characterizes Thrasymachus's argumentative oratory as "clean-cut and precise, formidable in invention and in giving his meaning distinct and striking expression." He taught pupils rhetoric, primarily. Evidence indicates that he was cognizant of requirements for all three kinds of oratory: deliberative, forensic, and epideictic. In his teaching, and in his several books, Thrasymachus stressed appeals to emotions, especially anger and pity. He was among the earliest writers on affective appeals in oratory.

According to Theophrastus, student and lecturer at Aristotle's Lyceum, Thrasymachus was founder of the middle style, a mode half-way between grand and plain. Dionysius commented on the Chalcedonian's use of that style:

> Thrasymachus's own diction, if it really was one of the sources of the intermediate manner, would seem to deserve commendation on the score of its intentions alone: it is a good sort of mixture, and has adopted just what was serviceable in the other two. (Sparshott 90)

The other two are the grand and plain. Dionysius quotes from one of Thrasymachus's political speeches; it is a long passage, typifying the intermediate or middle style (Usher 249, 251):

Gentlemen, I would have preferred to share in the political life of old, when young men were expected to remain silent, because their participation in debate was unnecessary and their elders managed the state's affairs efficiently. But since fate has assigned me to an age in which others rule the city and we obey them, but we ourselves suffer the disastrous consequences of their rule (for the worst of these are not the work of gods or of chance, but of human ministers), I am forced to speak. For a man who will allow himself to be continually exploited by anyone who wishes to, and will take the blame for other men's treachery and cowardice, is either a fool or a model of patient forbearance. We have had enough of the past and the change from peace to the danger of war: up to now we have constantly been hankering after yesterday and dreading tomorrow. Enough, too, of the change from concord to mutual hostility and turbulence. While everyone else is made arrogant and seditious by an excess of good fortune, this had a sobering effect upon us; but we have lost our heads when faced with misfortunes, which usually have a sobering effect upon others. What, therefore, is a man going to conclude or say when he is left to contemplate the present state of affairs with dismay, while at the same time thinking that he knows how to prevent its continuance into the future? The first thing I shall point out is that those politicians and others who are engaged in argument stand in a paradoxical relationship to one another, as is inevitable when men indulge in thoughtless wrangling. For, thinking that they express opposing views, they do not see that their policies are identical and that their opponents' speeches contain the same arguments as their own. Consider from the beginning the aims of both parties. The first object of contention is the ancestral constitution, that possession which all citizens hold most in common and which is very easy to find out about. Now for events which are beyond our knowledge we must rely on accounts provided by our ancestors; as to events which our senior citizens have actually witnessed, we must learn of these from their own lips.

Dionysius concluded that such was the sort of language used by Thrasymachus: "well-blended mixture of the two extremes, and an appropriate starting point for the study of both."

That accomplishment on style was significant, yet Thrasymachus's study of prose rhythms adds to his distinction as an innovator in rhetorical theory. Aristotle claimed that Thrasymachus discovered the *paean,* a rhythmic pattern of alternating sounds, short and elongated. Found by Thrasymachus to be appropriate to oratory, the paean provided aesthetic and emotional appeal, giving audiences pleasure and satisfaction. Too, it added variety when mixed with other forms of address.

In another accomplishment in style, Thrasymachus was one of the first theorists to study tropes and periodic style in speaking.

Regarding delivery, Aristotle observed that Thrasymachus and a few others were the only ones who had written anything on the topic.

Finally, it should be mentioned that Thrasymachus was outspoken on the function of law in society. This characteristic got him much attention from Plato in the *Republic,* though he is certainly more villain than hero in that book. Justice, Thrasymachus said, was no more than the advantage of the stronger. The powerful — the rulers — made laws that satisfied their own interests and ends. The weaker in society were constrained to accept laws as right and proper. With this belief on justice, Thrasymachus must be placed among those who adhered to the point of view that law rather than nature — convention rather than the way things naturally are — is the determiner of man's lot in life. Thrasymachus's position, whether assessed as realistic, pessimistic, or cynical, puts him in the company of Protagoras, Gorgias, and Prodicus.

3

ATHENIANS AND THE SOPHISTS

*D*espite their popularity and success as educators, the great sophists did become objects of criticism in Athens. Why? Why should anyone disapprove of people who provided useful learning? Basic to comprehension of the anti-sophist strictures is awareness of the fifth-century beliefs, ideologies, and interests challenged by the sophists' teaching.

Athens of that time incorporated an array of forces, many of which at one moment or another were in opposition to these professional teachers. Virtually every dimension of human thought and action was represented in reactions to the sophists: intellectual, political, social, moral, religious, educational, and economic. The striking presence of the sophists evoked response — negative and positive — from every quarter. As with innovators in any period of great change, they were controversial, both received and repudiated. It should not be surprising that members of this "modernist" group gave people reasons — minor or great — to be dubious, fearful, resentful, or antagonistic. The following catalog names some of the issues and positions that they encountered. Obviously, topics overlap.

A CHALLENGE TO TRADITIONALISTS

Traditionalists took the sophists as "progressives" — radical advocates of change — and contributors to a breakdown in moral values
that they, the "old guard," believed was occurring. In the friction
between the younger and older generations, the sophists occupied a
position between. But holders of conventional attitudes saw the
sophists as instigators of behavior in a new breed of citizen. The
sophists were sponsors of those ambitious heirs to the new democracy
and therefore were considered responsible for instability in the
culture. Promising training for better places in the community,
these professional teachers intruded upon established structures of
rearing the young and preparing them for life. They questioned
standing prerogatives. Formal "lessons" by clever — too clever —
itinerant strangers challenged the long-relied-upon family group
system, the *natural* learning of *association* that occurred in family
and community. The sophists' programs were divisive, coming as a
wedge between family and son. And the turning of settled practices
into topics for open discussion was found threatening, particularly
on questions of morality and codes of behavior.

In terms of our twentieth century, the conservative citizenry held
the sophists to be destroyers of natural authority, blind to obvious
distinctions between right and wrong, and easy on offenders against
community standards. They were subversive intellectuals and
professors: dangerous people in the community.

A THREAT TO ARISTOCRATS

Aristocrats — most of whom were traditionalists quite likely —
holding to a presumption of power by virtue of parentage or
position, interpreted the teaching of sophists as an assault on their
naturally derived status. They stood to lose this advantage if it
became the order that young men would be *taught* into gentility and
consequently into high political and social ranking. Doubtless many
fathers were torn between providing their sons the advantages of the
sophists' instruction and risking strife or other far-reaching losses.

Illustrative of one form of social comment by traditionalists and aristocrats on the sophists' presence in Athens are plays by Old Comedy writers, particularly Aristophanes. Below is a passage from his *Clouds*. A certain character (a "right thinker" — of the "old school") envisions a happy return to better days, when

> . . . you'll excel in the games you love well,
>   all blooming, athletic and fair:
> Not learning to prate as your idlers debate
>   with marvelous prickly dispute,
> Nor dragged into Court day by day to make sport
>   in some small disagreeable suit:

Instead you will go off to the playing fields —

>   and under the olives contend
> With your chaplet of reed, in a contest of speed
>   with some excellent rival and friend:
> All fragrant with woodbine and peaceful content,
>   and the leaf which the lime blossoms fling,
> When the plane whispers love to the elm in the grove
>   in the beautiful season of spring. [357]

Here is my modernized interpretation:

> Return to the old way, and you'll excel in respected, traditional Greek athletic contests — not learning to jabber on like those drones in debate over a certain hair-splitting or cute argument — nor fooling around in court in some dumb, quibbling dispute.
> Instead of all that rhetorical-democratic-sophistical wrangling — all that crap that they teach now and lay on the youth, it'll be back to the good old days of earning real glory: a time when gentlemen conducted civic affairs and settled matters in genteel fashion — when how you played the game counted most and life was tranquil.

The sophists were identified with the great and threatening changes occurring then.

RESENTMENT OF DEMOCRATS

Democrats, whose numbers increased in the fifth century, had reasons for being irritated by the sophists who cast their favors before sons of upper classes, for significant numbers of the pupils' families had oligarchical tendencies in government. Training potential political enemies, and thereby adding to their power, amounted to political interference and a show of preference. Too, the sophists were paid well for serving some of the high born. Thus their efforts were seen in one sense as an obstacle to democratic aims, despite philosophic compatibility.

Consider, too, the people unable to attend classes, for instance, those who could not afford them and those restrained by circumstances of time, place, or other condition. They had obvious reasons for resentment. Doubtless some of the unfortunates were represented among the democrats. Thus disgruntled democrats contributed to criticism of the sophists.

CONFLICTS OF IDEOLOGIES AND VALUES

Ideological opponents, those whose philosophical positions or views on teaching clashed with the sophists', apparently were not as large a group or as strong or vocal as their counterparts in the next century — Plato's time — yet they did exist, as that author reported in his dialogues. Among points at issue were the sophists' tenet that knowledge must necessarily be relative to the individual, the sophists' neglect of science, their recognition of probability as a guide to conduct, their pursuit of functional truths (as opposed to absolute), their emphasis on material success, and their alleged teaching of deceitfulness: teaching students to argue from any point of view and presumably making the worse appear the better reason.

If Socrates's observations in Plato's dialogues are at all representative of fifth-century conditions — in contrast to those of the fourth century in which Plato lived and wrote — the sophists clashed with contemporaries in daring to claim knowledge and to possess the ability to teach it to others. To intellectuals — particularly those of a Socratic bent — the professing of ability in imparting knowledge was a form of impudence, if not absurdity. Moreover, some objected to the sophists' collecting a fee for teaching, considered by their critics to be a demeaning and therefore a wrongful act.

XENOPHOBIC REACTIONS

Athenians fearing foreigners had ready-made grounds for opposition to the sophists, since the principal sophists of the fifth century, in particular the five treated here, were from other cities. Indeed, a case can be made for the assertion that the early sophists' alien status in Athens was the primary reason for indictment of them as a group. All Greeks — Thebans, Phocians, Argives, and others, as well as Athenians — were proud of their citizenship in a city. A force from without, felt to be a threat to their security or institutions, was met with provincial hostility or prejudice. More than a source of pride, citizenship was a guard to be held up. It was the base of a deeply felt identity to be defended, sometimes at great cost. The alien sophists doubtless gave sensitive citizens concern.

Incidentally, regarding the reception of citizens of foreign cities, it would be well to remember that the sophists quite obviously were held in high regard at home! — trusted as they were in representing their cities abroad. Clearly, in ancient Greece one's credibility and merit often were measured by the criterion of identity — alien or citizen.

CONFLICTS ON RELIGION

The sophists' teachings clashed with prevailing religious precepts. Greeks who were cognizant of their religious impulses as contrasted with common interpretations of the sophists' thought on religion felt the shock of the rationalism and were disturbed. Religion of the general population was based on nature, simple and unsophisticated. It was *felt*, by experience and observation of natural phenomena, and did not need intellectual cultivation. Certainly, it was bound up with superstitious practice and belief. The sophists' skepticism was taken as a challenge to beliefs, for example, that acts of the gods explained mysteries of weather, war, love, and the like. The sophists

opened the subject to academic examination and raised fundamental doubts about power of the gods. "If man is the 'measure of
all things,' is he above the gods?" Thus the sophists threatened ordinary theology and produced fearful reaction.

TARGET OF THE DISCONTENTED

Interpretations of the sophists' ways and ideas provided discon-
certed, defensive citizens with a locus for grievances. Any person
disenchanted by contemporary conditions found the high profile of
the sophists on social, moral, and educational subjects an available
and attractive target. Social disequilibrium, present all through the
fifth century, was intensely manifest during its final third, the
period of the Peloponnesian War — when the sophists flourished.
Losses experienced in times of crisis, poor economic conditions,
personal tragedy, or depression of spirit must needs be answered in
some way. Efforts must be made to achieve social and personal
homeostasis, to balance things. Perhaps the need is particularly
great in a society which is sensitive to determining or maintaining a
national or civic identity and effectively enforcing it abroad. Such
were the conditions and needs of the late fifth-century Athenians.
Too, untoward social conditions may motivate a yearning for return
to better days or an exorcising of sources of discontent, as Aristophanes's plays remind us. Of course, the imbalance in the fifth century to some extent had been contributed to by the sophists with
their relativistic and skeptical outlook, making it easier to associate
them with conditions generally. Also, we must acknowledge that in
crisis a people is likely to seek a vulnerable group on whom to project
self-doubts and fears. A case in point in the fifth century is the
behavior of the violent Cleon in his speech before the Athenian
Assembly in 427. In strident tones, he urged that body to vote for
execution of Mytilenaean citizens guilty of revolt, declaring arro-
gantly that anyone in the Assembly who dared to answer his charges
"must be some one who, under the inspiration of a bribe, elaborates
a *sophistical* [italics mine] speech in the hope of diverting you from
the point." And, "you are all at the mercy of your own ears, and sit
like spectators attending a performance of sophists." The speaker

— and certainly the historian Thucydides, who reported the speech — was aware of that audience's disposition. Cleon knew well the rhetorical force of his reference to a vulnerable group. Feelings about sophists were to be found in the community, latent in listeners' minds and to be exploited by the discontented or anxious. The main subject of this point is not Cleon but the availability of a useful commonplace: the sophists and what they variously represented to members of the Athenian Assembly and the general population, particularly in time of distress.

Notwithstanding the resentment occasioned by their presence in the community, the sophists served a willing clientele, and they left a significant intellectual legacy.

qual terms, thanks to development of rhetorical ability. Enforcing
e vision of what could be and coupling practical training to it, the
phists gave people not only a philosophical base for liberalizing
tlooks but also the specific skills for implementation. Authority
uld be challenged effectively; nature could be answered; change
s possible; political advancement and social mobility could be
lized.

The sophists structured a practical curriculum bent toward devel-
ment of *aretê,* including methods of building and defending a
e in the courts and advocating policy in the Assembly. They
ght people oratory and other arts for political success and
tural awareness. They gave valuable instruction in organization
hought in speeches, functional logic, employment of emotional
eals, analysis and use of language, and delivery of speeches.

y precept and example — principle and demonstration — they
e systems of persuasion available to people, meeting ignorance
clear instruction and direction. They enforced the knowledge
people could learn application of principles of rhetoric, that
were not gifts of an aristocratic few.

eir epistemology was functional: knowledge was for use in
ng needs as they arose and coming to good decisions. Thus
lessons in rhetoric were to the end of developing readiness,
rstanding audiences and situations, of discovering and decid-
n useful argument.

the process of learning rhetorical skills, the sophists' students
others affected by their teachings strengthened thought
ses; they developed sensitivity to ideas and relationships
them. For example, Gorgias's instruction in apagogic struc-
of argument doubtless led to awareness of significant mental
ions and reasoning patterns.

hey learned speaking skills, students were forced to ponder
motivations and attitudes. For instance, mastery of the
doctrine on adaptation to audience and situation led to in-
understanding of the values on which people acted and from
a broader, more sophisticated — perhaps more cosmopolitan
view. Greater self-understanding was an obvious reward.

CONTRIBUTIONS OF THE SOPHISTS

*O*f the number of approaches that one may take in acknowledging
sophists' rhetorical contributions, two present themselves most
insistently: (1) credit the sophists for influence in their time and
beyond or (2) credit them, and *express regret that they had not been
of a different sort.* The second approach prompts attachment of
conclusions like, "True, sophists were significant teachers, yet in the
final analysis their assumptions were superficial" or "Though their
ideas were useful in Athens and their subsequent influence great,
the sophists were not genuine philosophers." Such qualifying may be
offered to balance recognition with reservation, lest any appreciation be taken as validation of all sophists in all roles: as teachers,
scholars, *and* thinkers. But unfortunately, overcautious or limited
recognition discounts positive value and tends towards an ambi-
valence that does not satisfy. This account will take the first of the
two approaches in assessment — crediting for accomplishment — on
the premise that if the sophists had not been who they were and had
not behaved as they did, they would not have produced the results
for which they are commended. Too, one must remember that the
subject here is the sophists of the fifth century; they were quite a

different group from many of those who followed, a point of distinction not always respected in evaluations of the sophists.

Protagoras, Gorgias, Prodicus, Hippias, and Thrasymachus provided their contemporaries with new knowledge, useful skills, and liberalized attitudes. Their teaching affected everyone in the community, directly or indirectly. The purpose here is to name contributions of the fifth-century sophists, particularly to the theory and practice of rhetoric. But first, a brief general observation.

GENERAL CONTRIBUTIONS

Most significantly, the sophists introduced Athens — and the rest of Greece — to a new and vital philosophy. We would call it *humanism,* using the term in reference to *human* nature, interests, resources, society, ways of being, growth and development, and like matters. Forcibly challenging Ionian preoccupation with natural philosophy, they directed attention to human issues as a proper study, to the behavior and ethics of people. They brought about a consciousness of community and the use of the intellect in purposeful study of the culture. They stimulated awareness of political, social, and natural phenomena affecting people's lives and taught that influencing forces can be analyzed systematically and can be understood through use of a disciplined mind. They directed the power of their writing and teaching toward raising people's consciousness of their attributes as social creatures and of their identity as individuals. Each person had a mind capable of improvement; each person had potential for functioning effectively in the community.

The sophists put forward systems of learning and inquiry that were at once humanistic and practical. As scholars, they added to the subject matter of a number of areas, and they opened up new fields of knowledge for study by subsequent investigators. The breadth of their curricula reflects the extent of their inquiry.

The sophists categorized subject matter by giving names to areas of specialization: to rhetoric, grammar, use of synonyms in discourse, and logic. From their classifications came concepts,

principles, and disciplines which were accepted by s
lowed and which have persisted to this time.

As professional teachers, the sophists provided
education unavailable before their arrival. Offer
century sophists, though individually and irreg
constituted a "university curriculum," as writer
Werner Jaeger traces influences of sophists in the
vium (logic, rhetoric, and grammar) to the quadr
music, geometry, and astronomy) which togeth
seven liberal arts of medieval universities — an
origins of educational systems in our twentieth
"All in all," writes Will Durant in reference to
liberal arts, the sophists "must be ranked amon
tors in the history of Greece" (361).

RHETORICAL THEORY AND P

Protagoras, Gorgias, Prodicus, Hippias, and
rhetoric a prominent place in their programs.
tain rhetorical principles and expanded on
they carried the study immeasurably beyond
found it and bequeathed to succeeding theor
problems for examination; they stimulated
tions of rhetoric in the community, encourag
foundations and services, and gave explicit

Most of these sophists consistently upheld
vention in the nature-law controversy abo
conduct and potential. They taught that h
predetermined, that humankind could u
natural forces. The Greek people could us
themselves. They could be taught to condu
tively as orators and thereby ready thems
ness and standing in the community.

Training in persuasion gave encourage
ful of competing with "naturally gifted"
lished positions. Emerging leaders becar

Sophists were innovators in discovering and drawing attention to particular forms and elements of style, and through the power of instruction and effective personal demonstration they influenced adoption of rhythmic patterns, tropes, and other constructions. The work of Thrasymachus comes to mind here. By including poetic elements in rhetorical discourse, they endorsed a holistic view of discourse that did not distinguish between the aesthetic and functional. As an instance, Gorgias in "Helen" said, "I both deem and define all poetry as speech with meter." Evidences of such union can be seen in certain points of view prevalent today, e.g. in the writings of Kenneth Burke and Wayne Booth, who find rhetorical motive in all discourse.

Sophists were leaders in advocacy of verbal precision. And by teaching means of analyzing linguistic structures, they made their contemporaries aware of the workings and services of language. Prodicus's activities may give the best example. He strove to build a consciousness in language behavior — to remove mystery from the study, teaching that choices in language usage are critical and that standards can be set.

At least one sophist, Hippias, discovered memory techniques, taught memory improvement, and personally promoted the value of memorization in rhetorical practice.

The sophists countered naivete, ignorance, and innocence with a rhetorical view. They taught hard lessons about compelling suppositions in uses of persuasion: the rule of probability, the fact of issues in every proposition, the tough choices to be made in solution of rhetorical problems. From the sophists — most directly from Protagoras — people learned that one person's "truth" might not be another's, that positions are debatable, that the only way to "truth" is through examination of both sides; and, therefore, that effective advocacy is essential in the community.

In teaching people that they *of themselves* could be a force among their peers and that they had powers of choice, the sophists answered fifth-century thinking that credited natural forces for success or failure in rhetorical experience. *People* were responsible for their behavior, not the gods or nature; that, too, was reflective of the sophists' humanism. Thus, they were party to adding weight of responsibility to individual shoulders, to activation of conscience, to rhetorical maturity. In this significant effort the sophists were followed by Aristotle, whose *Rhetoric,* systematic and whole, seems in important ways to be an expansion of themes addressed by the fifth-century sophists. For example in studying Protagoras, one is struck by similarities in his and Aristotle's philosophies and realistic attitudes on uses of rhetoric. Both Aristotle and the sophists recognized rhetoric as a major source of power in the community.

The time in which these great teachers flourished, whether named the "Age of the Sophists" or the "Age of Illumination" or the "Age of Enlightenment" (Burnet 109, Bury 376-397, Guthrie 48), produced such changes in human thought and action as to influence profoundly the direction of future events in the history of humankind. It is not enough to say that the sophists' effect is seen in the works of the Attic Orators or that their presence is visible in writings of Thucydides, Euripides, Hippocrates, and possibly Aristotle — to name but four great writers of antiquity, or, with Mario Untersteiner, to say that the sophists must "be given the credit of having conceded to man the right to human life, human speech, and human thought" (xvi). No, the conclusion must be stronger, perhaps much like G. B. Kerferd's recommendation that the sophists be recognized as "a no less distinguished and important part of the achievement of Periclean Athens" than the regularly acknowledged great figures. The sophists were "important in their own right and important also in the history of philosophy" *(Sophistic Movement* 175-176).

5

PLATO AND THE IDEA OF SOPHISTRY

*T*he sophists were products of their time who taught and wrote for the people of that time. W. K. C. Guthrie concluded, they "were not scholars writing philosophical and scientific treatises for the future. They were rather teachers, lecturers and public speakers, whose aim was to influence their own age rather than to be read by posterity" (52-53). It is true that in responding to fifth-century conditions and issues — to questions on law, politics, religion, and human existence — and in seeking means of addressing the very real problems facing Greeks of that day, their concerns were immediate. And yet, as we know, they did find a wider audience, and the influence of their formulations went far beyond their own day. They were men of learning and educational purpose who built more effectively than they or their contemporaries knew.

PLATO'S PURPOSE

With such an understanding of aims and achievements of the fifth-century sophists, let's now examine purposes of the fourth-century Plato and draw a line of connotative distinction between the words "sophist" and "sophistry," that is, undo Plato's connection.

For it is Plato who is primarily responsible for the "historical untruth" (Finley 123) that has attainted the sophists, even to this day.

Agglomerating selected features of sophists' thoughts and their relationships with the people, Plato shaped a great figure of artfulness and used it as a model in promoting his moral philosophy. In so doing, he established the idea of "sophistry" and assured for the term a long-standing pejorative meaning. But though the sophist is his philosophical enemy, the citizens, perceived in ignorance and moral weakness, are to Plato the basic problem.

Passages in the *Republic** make the point:

> Do you really think, as people so often say, that our youth are corrupted by Sophists, or that private teachers of the art corrupt them in any degree worth speaking of? Are not the public who say these things the greatest of all Sophists, and do they not educate to perfection young and old, men and women alike, and fashion them after their own hearts? [492].
>
> Sophists . . . teach nothing but the opinion of the many, that is to say, the opinions of their assemblies. [493]

The result of Plato's writings is a master draft of the idea of sophistry. His is a fourth-century conception, founded on his indictment of public response to the appeal of those teachers of practical wisdom. Without evidence of a positive reception of the sophists by Athenians — without public acknowledgment of value in the sophists' offerings — Plato could not have built the case for his philosophy. The sophists, in their connection with the people, provided a neat target: worthy and popular, highly visible, vulnerable. Consider this relevant characterization of the sophist-citizen relationship which Plato included in the *Republic:*

> I might compare them [sophists] to a man who should study the tempers and desires of a mighty strong beast who is fed by him — he

*All quotations of Plato are Jowett translations, except Lindsay's (noted at occurrence), chosen for greater clarity and force. The bracketed numbers refer to sections in the edited Plato text, not to pages.

would learn how to approach and handle him, also at what times and from what causes he is dangerous or the reverse, and what is the meaning of his several cries, and by what sounds, when another utters them, he is soothed or infuriated; and you may suppose further, that when, by continually attending upon him, he has become perfect in all this, he calls his knowledge wisdom, and makes of it a system or art, which he proceeds to teach, although he has no real notion of what he means by the principles or passions of which he is speaking, but calls this honourable and that dishonourable, or good or evil, or just or unjust, all in accordance with the tastes and tempers of the great brute. Good he pronounces to be that in which the beast delights and evil to be that which he dislikes; and he can give no other account of them except that the just and the noble are the necessary, having never himself seen, and having no power of explaining to others the nature of either, or the difference between them, which is immense. [493]

It is a powerful and irrational human nature, says Plato, that motivates behavior of the sophists.

PLATO'S RHETORICAL STRATEGY

The sophist is Plato's convenient foe. He is depicted as a pretender, a false philosopher. He is a discredited being, one who espouses mere beliefs and opinions, while imitating the truthseeker. Deception is his art; appearances are his creations.

Plato's portrayal of immorality in the sophists serves in contrast to exalt his *philosopher*. It is the philosopher whom Plato idealizes: the dedicated, honest, intelligent seeker of real knowledge and truth.

The philosopher	*The sophist*
is a noble amateur,	is a cynical professional,
seeks knowledge and pursues the permanent and universal,	deals in opinion and probabilities and accepts the transitory,
is guided by reason and disciplined behavior,	relies on fallible senses and rhetorical gimmicks,

claims no answers to perennial and perplexing questions,	finds ready answers and solutions,
asks questions and tests ideas,	lectures and expounds,
sees order in the universe, evidence of a divine force, and	disrespectfully holds humankind to be the measure of all things and
is a trustworthy guide.	is an untrustworthy guide.

To achieve dominance of his philosophy and values — and to meet human fallibility as he perceived it, Plato brought to bear prodigious argumentative force and skillfully manipulated interactions that he included in his dialogues. Vlastos cites an instance in the *Protagoras,* in which the clever Plato "puts Protagoras into a tight spot, with no room for the exhibition of his dazzling paradoxes. Socrates slips in between the sophist and his admiring audience, precipitates a debate, fixes its topic, throws up swiftly a case for it, and leaves Protagoras no alternative but to fight on Socrates's own terrain. But why did Plato arrange things in this way? Because Socrates is the hero of this drama, and his interests dictate the choice of the subject matter" (xvi).

Certainly no one questions Plato's *rhetorical* power, though few use that particular adjective, preferring instead qualifiers like "literary" or "philosophical." But he was a rhetorical genius — with message, purpose, strategy, and immediate audience (and possibly a future audience, if one chooses the burden of defending that perspective).

It is in naming acts of the sophists and thereby inventing sharp distinctions and creative comparisons that Plato is most telling in advancing the superiority of his position. A prime and obvious example is his contrasting the sophists with the sterling personage of Socrates. Socrates's ethos, including cleverness and sagacity, argues Plato's case throughout many dialogues. In all scenes of interaction, Plato stands in association with Socrates, in contradistinction to the sophists. Against the Socratic paradigm, sophists appear as inferior thinkers and sometimes fools (though the worthy Protagoras in the dialogue bearing his name has moments as an admirable adversary).

Socrates the philosopher — wily and diligent pursuer of the good — is successful in every encounter with sophists. Alongside the right-thinking Socrates with his vexing but reliable question-and-answer method of inquiry, those "shallow thinkers" and makers of "long-winded speeches" lose any virility of reasoning that they might have possessed. In virtue, Plato's Socrates is everything that the sophists are not. More than an agent of truth, he is a citizen of Athens and identified with the community. But he makes no rash claims of knowledge or success in teaching. He stands for the highest in moral and intellectual goals, different from the success-minded tricky sophists. While the sure and confident Protagoras promises a prospective pupil,

> Young man, if you associate with me, on the very first day you will return home a better man than you came, and better on the second day than on the first, and better every day than you were the day before [*Protagoras* 318],

the diffident Socrates confesses, "I have no knowledge . . . no wisdom, small or great." [*Apology* 20 and 21]

Metaphorical strategy contributed significantly to Plato's rhetorical power. In the *Sophist,* for example, he names his subject a professional (paid) hunter. The sophist's art is a form

> which hunts animals, — living — land — tame animals; which hunts man, — privately — for hire, — taking money in exchange — having the semblance of education; and this is termed sophistry, and is a hunt after young men of wealth and rank. . . . [223]

Too, the sophist is a trader and a merchant of goods of the soul. His

> art may now be traced from the art of acquisition through exchange, trade, merchandise, to a merchandise of the soul which is concerned with speech [or reasoning] and the knowledge of virtue. [224]

It is the form of art

which either sells a man's own productions or retails those of others, as the case may be, and in either way sells the knowledge of virtue. . . . [224]

This again is sophistry, as Plato worked to fix the idea.

Elsewhere in the *Sophist,* Plato depicts his subject as an argumentative gymnast, a magician and imitator of true being, and a manufacturer of his own wares. In other dialogues, the sophist is a skillful dancer, inscrutable creature, juggler, sorcerer, physician of ignorance, and numerous other beings guilty of deception and unreliability.

Sarcasm and ridicule are additional resources used by Plato to characterize the sophists and their acts. In the *Protagoras* [310], Socrates chaffs that Protagoras will "make you as wise as he is himself" — if you influence him with money and persuasion. And, referring to the sophists' clever word-play, Socrates quizzically observes,

> The thoroughbred Sophists, who know all that can be known about the mind, and argue only out of the superfluity of their wits, would have had a regular sparring-match over this [topic of discussion], and would have knocked their arguments together finely. But you and I, who have no professional aims, only desire to see what is the mutual relation of these principles. . . . [*Theaetetus* 154]

Plato's reference to the sophists' alien status and itinerant habits doubtless capitalized on Athenian suspicion of foreign teachers and of their bold, confident presence in the city. As with most aliens in the city, the sophists' identity as foreigners had at times given them unwanted attention. Plato made a point of this part of their being, thereby naming them outlanders. In the *Euthydemus,* Crito asks Socrates about two *strangers,* who, he imagines, are "a new importation of Sophists." Specifically, "Of what country are they," and "what is their line of wisdom?" [271] Later in the dialogue Ctesippus talks with Socrates about the possibility of being "skinned by these foreigners" — these sophists. Socrates, in the *Timaeus,* himself makes the sophists' transient ways a criterion of judgment:

I am aware that the Sophists have plenty of brave words and fair conceits, but I am afraid that being only wanderers from one city to another, and having never had habitations of their own, they may fail in their conception of philosophers and statesmen, and may not know what they do and say in time of war, when they are fighting or holding parley with their enemies. [19]

Socrates touches on the issue of citizenship in the *Protagoras,* when he scolds a young gentleman on his associating with Protagoras:

But when the soul is in question, which you hold to be of far more value than the body, and upon the good or evil of which depends the well-being of your all, — about this you never consulted either with your father, or with your brother or with any one of us who are your companions. But no sooner does this foreigner appear, than you instantly commit your soul to his keeping. In the evening, as you say, you hear of him, and in the morning you go to him, never deliberating or taking the opinion of any one as to whether you ought to intrust yourself to him or not. . . . [313]

THE DIALOGUE AND SOCRATIC METHOD

Plato's chief method of furthering his message is consistent with the message and augments it. The dialogues in which Socrates participates are argumentative in both *form* and *substance,* a point discussed at greater length in Appendix A. Distinguished by Plato from procedures of the sophists, Socrates's system is built on innocence of certainty, reflecting the master's humility and a "genuine philosopher's" doubts on his ability to teach virtue and good behavior. Socratic reserve characterizes both thought and system. As evidenced in the *Apology,* Socrates neither knows nor thinks he knows, and therefore, is wiser than one who knows nothing but thinks he knows.

Socrates in the *Meno* holds that "all enquiry and all learning is but recollection" of knowledge stored in the soul: "there is no teaching, but only recollection"; thoughts in the soul "only need to be awakened into knowledge by putting questions" to a person *(passim)*. As questioner of a willing respondent, Socrates is a midwife to the birth of truth. His is not a pedagogy, *per se,* but a process of learning through cooperative logical analysis: dialectical interaction. To readers, it is an engaging form of self-discovery in which they become involved as they harken to the unfolding of events.

In vigorously contrasting Socrates's modesty and question-and-answer method with the sophists' claim to knowledge and their long speeches, Plato found a potent stratagem in furthering his purpose. As he structured his dialogues,

> The sophists' way was *easy* but the gain *tawdry;* Socrates's way was *difficult* but the gain *precious.*
> The sophists *pleased* with *answers;* Socrates *agitated* with *questions.*
> The sophists' role was to *teach sham to* pupils; Socrates's to *discover truth with* them.
> They *reinforced opinions;* he *exposed ignorance.*
> The sophists' method was *rhetorical;* his *dialectical.*
> They *persuaded;* Socrates *provoked.*

Further, the dramatic interaction of two minds engaging in a Socratic dialogue is in itself appealing. In setting up the give-and-take between humble Socrates and a responsive partner, Plato engages the reader in an exciting intellectual game. The reader enjoys going along with Socrates as he humiliates pretenders to knowledge and moves step by step toward revelation of truth. At the end of an exchange, the reader shares the satisfaction of resolution or discovery. Plato's representation of Socratic methodology is an ingeniously conceived rhetorical process that allowed him to ingratiate himself — his philosophy — with the reader, creating identification with the exemplary Socrates and dissociation from his philosophical opponents.

When run through the Socratic system of inquiry, the behavior of the sophists comes out debased and is indicted as "sophistry." Plato makes the process adversarial, putting properties of the sophists in a bill of particulars or charges against them. On trial are sophists' points of view, methods, goals, values — their worth in the community. The plaintiff's examination, conducted by the supremely unpretending Socrates, features relentless questioning and probing, critical testing of statement, checking of premises and evidence — comprising a purposeful, disciplined, and rational arraignment and exposé of falseness in being.

Socratic-Platonic use of dialogue as strategy comes out in a passage in the *Republic*. In discussion with Glaucon on how to engage with Thrasymachus, Socrates recognizes the peculiarly forensic character of his system and argues its comparative merits. His argument is attractive:

> . . . if we match ourselves against him and give speech for speech, enumerating the advantages of justice, and he speaks a second time, and we speak yet again, then we must add up and measure the advantages enumerated by each party in each speech, and we shall need a jury to decide between us. But if we allow our previous form of inquiry, arguing till we come to an agreement, then we shall be at the same time jury and advocates. [348] (Lindsay translation)

By controlling the interaction through the use of the "previous form of inquiry" — dialogue — and ruling out speech after speech, they will avoid the need to consult with anyone outside themselves: they will not have to bother with an audience of people with ideas of their own.

In a number of dialogues, Plato called into question "eristical" methods of sophists. The Eristics of Megara were contemporaries of Plato, a once-respected school of philosophers whose methods had deteriorated into a kind of shoddy dialectic. Instead of seeking truth, as did Socrates, the Eristics sought to win arguments or to argue for the sake of arguing. In the *Sophist,* Plato named the sophists a "money-making species of the Eristic." They were "Disputatious, controversial, pugnacious, combative." Plato advanced this image in other dialogues as well, among them the *Theaetetus* and *Euthydemus*. In these writings, he was less concerned with laying out the sophists' inclination to make long, evasive speeches — as distinct from Socrates's brief and direct statements — than with asserting the sophists' alleged predisposition to wrangle and quibble. So indiscriminate and trenchant is Plato's characterization of the sophists — if not excessive — that one must wonder about his intent. Was he motivated by disenchantment with the group of Megaric philosophers who had taken up eristics (Burnet 230–232, Warrington viii)? Was that the instigation, for instance, of his colorful revelation of eristical nonsense in the *Euthydemus* (a dialogue in which he did not "name names": did not give historical names to subjects of his criticism)? Are the great sophists of the fifth century victims by association in Plato's generalized indictment of eristical "sophists" of the fourth? Whether his immediate subject was inferior philosophers, generally, or sophists specifically — or both undistinguished, or any other person or group, he calls them *sophists,* and reproves them. In these dialogues, particularly the *Sophist, Theaetetus,* and *Euthydemus,* Plato makes his target — those philosophical and moral weaklings — such an "easy shot" that one wonders whether he is carelessly or purposefully indistinct in reference to his subject.

Further, it must be asked whether Plato's sophists are figures used in certain dialogues as whipping posts for one of his particular controversies, for instance his conflict with Isocrates, successful teacher of rhetoric and staunch rival. To suit his ends of the moment, Plato may be guilty of associating current issues with persons long passed from the scene (Segal 138, Burnet 108). And it would be incorrect of us to read fourth-century grievances back into an earlier time and thereby lose sight of good works. In any event, Plato's attachment of sophists to eristics contributed immeasurably to criticism of all sophists and to molding his idea of sophistry.

IN THE FINAL ANALYSIS

Thus Plato portrayed the sophist: the teacher who dared to promise success and collect a fee, the suspected foreigner, the pseudo philosopher, the quibbler, the deceiver, the seducer whose actions revealed the moral weakness in human nature. *The central character in Plato's dialogues is humankind, whose being the sophist but mirrors and exploits.* To put forth his mighty premises, Plato selected from among available materials and cast two great opposing figures — SOCRATES and THE SOPHIST. He enlisted them to represent two sharply contrasting worlds, placing them face to face in dialectical interaction to demonstrate fundamental distinctions.

In that proceeding, he formulated his idea of sophistry and made it stick.

The dialogues were extraordinarily effective in promoting Plato's thought. His matchless dramatizations have been among the most authoritative works in world literature. Ironically, his power derived from the very source that the sophists made the core of their teaching: usages of rhetoric. Indeed, Plato is among the most influential rhetors of history, and his works might well serve as models of rhetorical practice. Though Platonism no longer enjoys its former position of dominance, the dialogues continue to carry meaning and convey a powerful conception.

While recognizing Plato's pre-eminence in the history of ideas, we would err to allow diminishment or depreciation of the sophists' great legacy. Giving credit to the former need not demand denial of the latter. Influences of the sophists are easy to appreciate, even without benefit of extant writings of length. The sophists have left us true value, in their unique and substantial contributions to western thought and to the history of rhetorical theory and practice.

The Platonic — the traditional — interpretation of the idea of sophistry is far removed from the ideas and behavior of Protagoras, Gorgias, Prodicus, Hippias, and Thrasymachus — perhaps as far removed as Plato's world was from theirs — or from ours. Certainly, we in these times should remember that our faith in democratic institutions and practice, freedom of choice, education for active citizenship, and uses of rhetoric is more representative of the sophists than of their mighty critic.

Finally, we would do well to recall that without the antecedence of the sophists, Greece and the world would have known neither Socrates nor his best pupil — nor the pupil's best pupil! And the greatest imagination cannot project the character of western civilization without a Plato and an Aristotle.

Appendices

The Issue of Speech Length in Plato's Attack on the Sophists

*P*lato makes his complaint against the sophists in a number of dialogues, but perhaps most trenchantly in the *Euthydemus* and in the *Sophist*. In the latter, he names the sophist a hunter of young men who takes money for the semblance of education; he is a trader in goods of the soul, one who sells the knowledge of virtue; he is an argumentative gymnast and an imitator of true being. Such are selected points of Plato's brief. But in other dialogues, especially in the *Protagoras,* he chooses to confront the sophists on their mode of discoursing, making speech length an issue.

My purpose here is to explore the conflict on this question, observing that *form* in Plato's argument against the sophists is essential to *substance.*

DIALOGUE

Most of Plato's writings are in dialogue form. The process is dialectical, and in ideal characterization, consists of reasoning to separate truth from error. In central position is Socrates, the great questioner and the most celebrated practitioner of dialogue. Ostensibly, the purpose of dialectic is not to defeat others but to sweep away irrelevant material and produce essences of ideas or an absolute or universal premise: on the meaning of virtue, for example. Success requires commitment and cooperation of participants. Aristotle names Zeno of Elea (ca. 490–ca. 420) as founder of the dialectical method (Kerferd 59). Zeno's use of it was in discovering "the pure soul of science," and the system provided him "true objectivity" as he quested for scientific laws and definitions (Hegel 1:261f). Interestingly, Zeno visited Athens when he was about forty years old (Burnet 82), a time when Socrates may have been in his early twenties. We do not know if the two had direct contact or whether Socrates's adoption of dialectic is to be explained through Zeno's intermediate influence. In any event, Plato knew the methodology from his association with Socrates, and he put it to service in his writings, as representative of Socrates's practice.

But not all dialogic interaction is true dialectic or reliable in seeking truth, certainly not in Plato's view. For example, the Megarics of the fourth century used a kind of dialogue called *eristic* which had as its purpose not a search for the good or true but victory in debate. In was argument for the sake of argument, often including purposeful use of fallacy and tricks. It epitomizes the kind of behavior portrayed and condemned by Plato in the *Euthydemus*. Another process assuming the form of dialogue is *antilogic,* a mode of philosophical debate in which antithetical positions are held by the participants in an exchange of questions and answers. The aim of each person in antilogic is to expose contradictions in the position of the adversary and cause him to reject his own position or to accept both his and the other person's position (Kerferd 63–64). Antilogic is akin to dialectic, and examples are found in selected dialogues of Plato. In the *Lysis,* for instance, Plato has Socrates discover that the greatest friendship is of opposites. Working to uncover contradictions, participants in antilogic may indeed come to seemingly odd conclusions, an example being that persons most opposed to one another are the most friendly, for "everything desires not like but that which is unlike," as the weak require aid of the strong. Notwithstanding his occasional use of antilogic as a "first step," Plato's preference is for a

purer dialectic, a method not seeking solely to discover verbal incon-
sistencies (Kerferd 59-67). And in development of thought, as we
shall see, he preferred the shorter mode of speaking to the longer.

LONG SPEECHES

Democracy was established in Athens in the fifth century.
Accordingly, it was a time of deciding on the utility of methods of
discourse to meet needs of given situations. But by the time of
the older sophists — Protagoras, Gorgias, Prodicus, Hippias, and
Thrasymachus — participants in community life had determined
that deliberations in courts and the legislative assembly required
longer speeches. Protagoras presumably was the first person to offer
regular instruction on preparing for forensic and political speaking.
Though he and other sophists, Gorgias for instance, reportedly were
capable of employing both short and long forms of address, they
definitely found greater effect in treating a topic at length and
without constant interruption. Moreover, the longer speech was the
sophists' chief means of teaching.

THE CLASH

The best evidence of the conflict between specialists of the two
oral forms is given by Plato in the *Protagoras*. The scene is the home
of a wealthy Athenian where a number of men have gathered to talk.
The sophists Prodicus and Hippias are there. Protagoras is there,
too, having arrived in Athens just two days earlier. It is a special
event for all, including Socrates who is anxious to meet and engage
the famous sophist of Abdera. In their exchange, form becomes a
major point of difference, with Socrates insisting that Protagoras
"shorten his answers, and keep to the point. . . . For discussion is
one thing, and making an oration is quite another." Protagoras is
reluctant to yield, asking, "Shall I answer what appears to me to be
short enough, or what appears to you to be short enough?"

In the argument over the form of discourse, the competitors reveal basic distinctions between their respective goals and beliefs.
Socrates's aim is not to profess but to seek unity in thought through

direct interrogation. The form of the process — and his management of it — are necessary to his effectiveness. The sure indication of success is the assent of his respondent.

Early in the dialogue, Protagoras makes a speech, seeking to convince Socrates and the others that virtue can be taught. His method is to develop arguments in detail. A main premise of his case is that Athenians — a wise and experienced people — are of the opinion that virtue may be taught, for obviously that is what they have been doing. That has been the practice of the people of Athens; over the years they have determined that virtue comes not from nature but from instruction. Such is the rule of social necessity (see Havelock 194), a conclusion that Protagoras can best demonstrate with a lengthy speech, which he does.

But Socrates, wanting to proceed in a manner that can reduce all matters to true essences, will trust no proposition save that resulting from dialectic — and only if he can carefully guide the interaction, in dialogue. He neither uses nor seeks general opinion, for it is unreliable and must be rejected. Protagoras, on the other hand, respects and depends on opinion. What counts is the lamp of experience; it is the stuff of his discourse. Eric Havelock's perspective is compelling in this context. He claims that in coming to decide things, both Plato — who is never detached from the material of his dialogues — and the sophists seek good and useful ends. The point of difference is in Plato's cosmic criteria: his demanding universal and timeless applicability. The sophists' epistemology is practical, formulated to discover correct decisions "at the point of immediate application where something has to be done" (203-205).

A closer examination of passages in the *Protagoras* will provide additional light on philosophical differences between Socrates and sophists and on the formal strategies Plato employs in advancing his ideas. First, it is apparent that Plato's Socrates must dominate, which of course he does in all dialogues. He is never bested. In the dialogue under discussion, Protagoras, presented as a learned and self-confident teacher, holds his own in the first phases of the encounter. But when the audience cheers one of Protagoras's longer and appealing statements — when the audience finds itself in a *rhetorical* mode and behaves accordingly—Socrates feels constrained to ask for short answers. Knowing that his goal can be reached in no other way, he insists that Protagoras adopt the "more compendious method." Equally firm, proud Protagoras replies that his purpose requires longer speaking: if on other occasions "I had followed the method of disputation which my adversaries desired, as you would want me to do, I should have been no better than another, and the name of Protagoras would have been nowhere." Socrates might say the same of his status as derived through his method.

Perceiving Protagoras's strong stand, Socrates declares that he will argue in no other way but his own. And he decides to leave the house, announcing, "I have an engagement which will prevent my staying longer to hear you at greater length. . . . I will depart." At this point, Prodicus and Hippias suggest compromises, one of which is to appoint an arbiter who will keep watch over speech length. But Socrates will not accept that and counters with the suggestion that *everyone* keep an eye on the participants' conduct. The discussion does go on, and Protagoras, "though very much against his will, was obliged to agree that he would ask questions" and give "short replies." He has felt the pressure and defers to group interests in having the talking continue.

It had to be settled in Socrates's favor. Socrates's purpose and advantage depended on dialogue — not to mention his management of it. His objective and Plato's must have congruence. Though he has Socrates express petty denunciation of the sophists for their speaking at tiresome length, Plato does more than air a minor gripe. Plato distinguishes characters of the philosopher and sophist: the one being single in purpose, not responsive to audience importunation or opinion, not accepting compromise or adjustment, but remaining steadfast as a seeker of verity; the other acknowledging popular will, making significant compromise in position, and agreeing to go along with interests of the generality. Reading along, we see that Protagoras is faithful to the agreement, but Socrates, of all people, is unable to deny rhetorical impulse and makes several long speeches — to which Plato has no one objecting. And though, as agreed, Protagoras takes the lead in the questioning, the power soon comes to reside with Socrates — with Plato. That, too, is inevitable. Unrestrained Platonic strategy overrides more subtle Socratic diffidence; Socrates *tells* more than he *asks*. The reader senses an insistence and force, much as in the pressing peroration of a speech that follows from more moderately styled thought.

From this point (about four-fifths though the dialogue) to the end, the event belongs to Plato, unmistakably. Protagoras becomes a resigned yes man. Working smoothly to get Socrates's point across, Plato gives Protagoras the attitude of a rehabilitated rebel who has learned the right way and the right words to say. Protagoras compliantly answers "yes" at least ten times to queries of Socrates — and many more times with "certainly," "I agree," "true," "you are right," and other forms of assent. This is Plato the graceful and assured rhetor at work. His authority is manifest, and the dialogue, without break or check, rhythmically flows as he would have it. But this is one of those dialogues with an untidy conclusion. It ends with Socrates expressing himself on some matters and hoping that he and Protagoras can meet again some evening, to clear up remaining questions.

As was noted in Chapter Five, Plato gives us a revealing statement in the *Republic* on strategic use of dialogue in argumentation. Socrates tells Glaucon that the only way to convince the erring Thrasymachus of the truth about justice is to use the question-and-answer mode of discourse. Otherwise a set speech by Thrasymachus would necessarily occasion a set replying speech which would provoke Thrasymachus to speak again, and on it would go. Such a procedure eventually would call for a jury to decide the merits of the respective arguments, Socrates observes. No jury is needed, Socrates tells Glaucon, for a dialogue requires only that the adversaries reach agreement: "we shall be at the same time jury and advocates."

We shall be jury and advocates. "We are a multitude," might be the paraphrase. No other agency is needed, as Plato would structure the process. In this comparative evaluation of methods, he makes obvious his philosophical dispute with the sophists and all others who appreciate uses of rhetoric and speechmaking. First is acknowledgment that arguments of a long speech invite refutation; people with opposing views will be heard. Second is acknowledgment that juries — audiences — are the final arbiters when controversy is free; indeed, they are a force in other rhetorical functions including invention of argument. Of course, Plato could not sanction a procedure of this sort. As Havelock noted,

> The material of discursive discussion is contributed by giving voice to the common opinions, attitudes and prejudices of men. Any creative results achieved, or any formalization of conclusions or decisions, are still a consensus of that kind of opinion. Plato will have none of it. (213)

Plato rejects the fifth-century Athenian decisions on democratic usages, on the opportunity to decide matters in a free and full debate.

In contrast, the conclusions of dialectic need not be fully demonstrated; "it holds good because it is accepted by the other party to the discussion. The whole fabric depends on the agreement of the two parties. . . ." (Burnet 164). It is a closed, self-sufficient system, functioning best when regulated by strict rules, with the respondent "not allowed to ask other questions or to boggle at the form of those put to him" (Burnet 134-135).

Rhetorical interaction, necessarily carrying *social* regulation, is rejected for the dialectical. As Plato's most illustrious pupil was to acknowledge a half-century later — and as Plato knew well — in choosing rhetoric, one hazards expression of audience will: it is the hearer, said Aristotle, "that determines the speech's end and object" (*Rhetoric* 1358b). Disciplined and skillful use of dialogue is more certain to yield value, Plato believed. In conforming to that system, participants avoid most of the distractions incurred in general-audience involvement as well as the risk of unmanageable dissent.

Moreover, structured typically with but two people interacting in a given episode, the question-and-answer method does not necessitate extensive audience adaptation, for there is less diversity of position. And either the participants agree on the regimen or the encounter is canceled. Rhetorical exchange requires accepting and coming to terms with a multiplicity of predispositions.

Fundamental to the points of difference, then, are two profoundly conflicting mentalities: democratic and authoritarian — one needing and trusting popular will and the other denying it. George Kennedy is convincing in his statement that the longer form of address was a product of democracy: a speech with reasoning, careful arrangement, and the like, "together with an attempt to secure attention and good will from ordinary citizens, and a conclusion designed to drive home the crucial points" (*Art of Persuasion* 42). In contrast, the dialogue is fundamentally an interrogation built on prescribed rules which give all control to the questioner and little to the respondent. The respondent is allowed scant opportunity to elaborate his thought. Further, says Havelock, "the questioner knows where he is going, and is going to direct his questions in that direction, and already possesses in his mind the main framework of ideas which the process is to expose bit by bit" (209). The Platonic-Socratic way demands obedience to form and leadership; neither purpose nor utility are derived from general consultation or choice.

Thus form and substance unite. The *absolutist* position, here observed in Plato's case against the sophists, finds consonance and agency in the dialogical short form of oral address. To the end of maintaining control, leadership is invested with dominant authority. Regulating all of its functions, the system rigidly restricts discussion, insists upon brief statement, denies refutation, arbitrarily acknowledges only the judgments it produces, and remains idealistically detached in seeking after the value it names as permanent.

The *democratic* idea enjoys congruity with the long speech — with form more obviously rhetorical. It accommodates free expression, extended argument, choice and management of thought — subject only to *social* regulation, necessary cooperation and consensus, refutation, flexibility of behavior, popular judgment, and a practical adaptable *episteme* for particular ends.

Applied to the question of final authority in the disposition of ideas, Protagoras's famous pronouncement, "Man is the measure of all things," becomes strikingly consistent with Aristotle's "the hearer determines." The audience is the source of power in true rhetorical interaction.

B

Gorgias's "Encomium of Helen": A Model Speech

Gorgias doubtless wrote this speech of respect for Helen, one of legendary history's most beautiful women, as a model piece of rhetoric, illustrating use of reasoning, clear structure, and his peculiar, captivating style. Helen also happened to be the wife of Menelaus, and the question has arisen about her possible "involvement" in her abduction. Was she attracted to the young prince who took her to Troy? After examining four possible reasons for Helen's departure — love, persuasion, force, or divine action, Gorgias concludes that Helen herself is blameless.

The reader should observe that the translator, La Rue Van Hook (122-123), chose to omit several parts of the speech, some of which reveal Gorgias's views on the power of persuasion. In omitted parts (see the Kennedy translation) Gorgias reasons that Helen "might have come under the influence of speech, just as if ravished by the force of the mighty." In showing the power of speech upon the soul, Gorgias turns to analogy: for just as some drugs "bring an end to disease and others to life, so also is the case of speeches," for "some distress, others delight, some cause fear, others make the hearers bold, and some drug and bewitch the soul with a kind of evil persuasion." Among other analogies used by Gorgias to build his case is one on impressions received through sight: "It has happened that people, after having seen frightening sights, have also lost presence of mind for the present moment; in this way fear extinguishes and excludes thought." Through vision Helen may have been charmed by the prince: "it is natural for the sight to grieve for some things and to long for others, and much love and desire for many objects and figures is engraved in many men." Thus Gorgias in his oral exercise exonerates Helen. Gorgias's speech follows:

1. Embellishment to a city is the valor of its citizens; to a person, comeliness; to a soul, wisdom; to a deed, virtue; to discourse, truth. But the opposite to these is lack of embellishment. Now a man, woman, discourse, work, city, deed, if deserving of praise must be honored with praise, but if undeserving must be censured. For it is alike aberration and stultification to censure the commendable and commend the censurable.

2. It is the duty of the same individual both to proclaim justice wholly, and to declaim against injustice holily, to confute the detractors of Helen, a woman concerning whom there has been uniform and universal praise of poets and the celebration of her name has been the commemoration of her fame. But I desire by rational calculation to free the lady's reputation, by disclosing her detractors as prevaricators, and by revealing the truth to put an end to error.

3. That in nature and nurture the lady was the fairest flower of men and women is not unknown, not even to the few, for her maternity was of Leda, her paternity immortal by generation, but mortal by reputation, Tyndareus and Zeus, of whom the one was reputed in the being, the other was asserted in the affirming; the former, the greatest of humanity, the latter, the lordliest of divinity.

4. Of such origin she was endowed with godlike beauty, expressed not suppressed, which inspired in many men many mad moods of love, and she, one lovely person, assembled many personalities of proud ambition, of whom some possessed opulent riches, others the fair fame of ancient ancestry; others the vigor of native strength, others the power of acquired wisdom; and all came because of amorous contention and ambitious pretention.

5. Who he was, however, who won Helen and attained his heart's desire, and why, and how, I will not say, since to give information to the informed conduces to confirmation but conveys no delectation. Passing over in my present discourse the time now past, I will proceed to the beginning of my intended discussion and will predicate the causes by reason of which it was natural that Helen went to Troy.

6. For either by the disposition of fortune and the ratification of the gods and the determination of necessity she did what she did, or by violence confounded, or by persuasion dumbfounded or to Love surrendered. If, however, it was against her will, the culpable should not be exculpated. For it is impossible to forestall divine disposals by human proposals. It is a law of nature that the stronger is not subordinated to the weaker but the weaker is subjugated and dominated by the stronger; the stronger is the leader while the weaker is the entreater. Divinity surpasses humanity in might, in sight, and in all else. Therefore, if on fortune and the deity we must visit condemnation, the infamy of Helen should find no confirmation.

7. But if by violence she was defeated and unlawfully she was treated and to her injustice was meted, clearly her violator as a terrifier was importunate, while she, translated and violated, was unfortunate. Therefore, the barbarian who verbally, legally, actually attempted the barbarous attempt, should meet with verbal accusation, legal reprobation and actual condemnation. For Helen who was violated and from her fatherland separated and from her friends segregated should justly meet with commiseration rather than with defamation. For he was the victor and she was the victim. It is just therefore to sympathize with the latter and anathematize the former.

8. But if it was through logos's reception and the soul's deception it is not difficult to defend the situation and forefend the accusation, thus. Logos is a powerful potentate, who with the frailest, feeblest frame works wonders. For it can put an end to fear and make vexation vanish; it can inspire exultation and increase compassion.

9. I will show how this is so. For I must indicate this to my hearers for them to predicate. All poetry I ordain and proclaim to be composition in meter; the listeners of which are affected by passionate trepidation and compassionate perturbation and likewise tearful

lamentation, since through discourse the soul suffers, as if its own, the felicity and infelicity of property and person of others.

10. Come let us turn to another consideration. Inspired incantations are provocative of charm and revocative of harm. For the power of song in association with the belief of the soul captures and enraptures and translates the soul with witchery. For there have been discovered arts twain of witchery and sorcery, which are consternation to the heart and perturbation to art.

15. Now, it has been shown that, if Helen was won over by persuasion, she is deserving of commiseration, and not condemnation. The fourth accusation I shall now proceed to answer with a fourth refutation. For if love was the doer of all these deeds, with no difficulty will she be acquitted of the crime attributed to her. The nature of that which we see is not that which we wish it to be but as it chances to be. For through the vision the soul is also in various ways smitten.

19. If, then, the eye of Helen, charmed by Alexander's [Paris's] beauty, gave to her soul excitement and amorous incitement, what wonder? How could one who was weaker, repel and expel him who, being divine, had power divine? If it was physical diversion and psychical perversion, we should not execrate it as reprehensible but deprecate it as indefensible. For it came to whom it came by fortuitous insinuations, not by judicious resolutions; by erotic compulsions, not by despotic machinations.

20. How, then, is it fair to blame Helen who, whether by love captivated, or by word persuaded, or by violence dominated, or by divine necessity subjugated, did what she did, and is completely absolved from blame?

21. By this discourse I have freed a woman from evil reputation; I have kept the promise which I made in the beginning; I have essayed to dispose of the injustice of defamation and the folly of allegation; I have prayed to compose a lucubration for Helen's adulation and my own delectation.

C

Prodicus's "Choice of Heracles": A Moral Lesson

*U*pon occasion, Prodicus would offer his lesson on ethics and moral goodness in which the popular legendary hero Heracles (Hercules) faces a major choice in life. Prodicus's audiences were large, Xenophon reported (38–40).

[Prodicus:] When Heracles was passing from boyhood to adolescence, when young men become their own masters and make clear whether they will turn in life onto the road of virtue or onto the road of evil, he went off and sat by himself in peace. He was at a loss as to which road to take. He saw two tall women approaching. One was lovely to see and by nature lively and forthright. Her body was adorned with purity, her eyes with modesty, and her bearing with temperance. She wore white. The other was plump and fleshy. She had painted her face to make her complexion whiter and redder than it really was. Her figure was gotten up to be taller than nature had made it. Her eyes were made up to give her a bold stare. She desired to display her beauty. She kept looking about her to see who was looking at her, and she often gazed at her own reflection. When they came closer to Heracles, the first woman went on unchanged. The other, eager to outdo her companion, rushed up to Heracles and said, "I see, Heracles, that you are in doubt as to which road to take in life. Make me your friend and I shall lead you along the easiest and most pleasant road. No delight will go untasted. You will live a life without hardship. First of all, you will take no thought for wars or troubles. Instead, your concern will be what choice food or drink you should find; what you should see or hear or touch or smell to delight you; what youths you would most enjoy associating with; how you may have the sweetest sleep; and how to get all this with the least labor. Should the suspicion ever arise that you lack the power of get this, don't be afraid that I will lead you through miserable discomforts of soul and body to win them! No! You will reap the fruits of other men's work. You will keep from nothing from which you could have gain. To my associates I give the power to profit any way and every way." When Heracles heard this, he asked, "Woman, what is your name?" She said, "My friends call me Happiness, but those who hate me disparage me with the name Evil."

Meanwhile the other woman approached him and said, "I come to you, Heracles, because I know your parents, and because I carefully observed your character during your childhood. As a result of this, I hope that, if you take the road that leads to me, you will become the noble doer of fine and holy deeds and that I shall appear even more honored and more famed for good. I shall not, however, deceive you by an introduction about pleasure. Instead I shall explain things truthfully, as the gods ordained them. The gods give men nothing noble and good unless men work and toil. If you want the gods to be propitious, you must serve the gods. If you want to be loved by friends, you must do good to your friends. If you desire to be honored by a state, you must help the state. If you ask to be admired by all of Greece for your virtue, you must try to aid Greece. If you wish the earth to bear fruit in abundance, you must cultivate the land. If you think that you should be enriched by cattle, you must care for the cattle. If you are eager to grow great through war and wish to be able to liberate your friends and overcome your enemies, you must learn the art of war from experienced men, and you must practice how to use it. If you want to have a strong body, you must train your body to serve your mind and exercise it with toil and sweat."

. . . Evil interrupted and said, "Do you realize, Heracles, how hard and long is the road to joy which this woman describes? I shall lead you along an easy and short road to happiness."

Virtue replied, "Wretched woman, what good thing do you possess? What pleasure do you know about? You are not willing to do anything to gain goodness or pleasure. You don't even wait to want pleasures, but before you feel any desire, you fill yourself full. You eat before you are hungry. You drink before you are thirsty. So as to eat pleasantly, you contrive to obtain cooks. To drink well, you prepare expensive wines and run around looking for snow in the summer. To sleep well, you not only get soft covers, but even footstools for your beds. You desire sleep not because you have worked hard, but because you have nothing to do. Before you need to, you arouse lust by every sort of means, and you use men like women. This is the way you educate your friends: by night you assault them and by day you sleep away the best hours. Though you are immortal, you were cast out from the gods; you are not honored among good men. You never hear the sweetest of all sounds: praise of yourself. You never see the sweetest of all sights: your own good work. Who would believe anything you said? Who would give you anything when you need it? What sensible man would dare to be one of your band of worshipers? For when your followers are young, their bodies are weak; and when they grow older, their souls are without sense. In their youth they are sleek and brought up without work. In their old age, they are dried up and go about with great effort; they are ashamed of what they did and are burdened with what they are doing. In their youth, they ran riot among pleasures and stored up bitter hardships for their old age.

"I am a companion of the gods. I associate with good men. There is no good deed, either divine or human, without me. I am honored most of all by the gods and men to whom I am related; I am a beloved fellow worker among craftsmen, a faithful guardian of householders, a blessed protector of slaves, a good assistant in peacetime labors, a sure ally in wartime deeds, and the best partner in friendship. For my friends, the enjoyment of food and drink is pleasant and painless, because they abstain until they desire them. Their sleep is sweeter than the sleep of the idle; they are not annoyed when they wake and they do not neglect their duties because of sleep. The young rejoice in praise from their elders; the older men delight in the respect of the young. They remember with pleasure the deeds of their youth and they enjoy their present activities. Through me, they are friends of the gods; beloved by friends, honored by their native land. When their allotted end comes, they do not lie unhonored and forgotten, but they are remembered and praised forever. O Heracles, child of good parents, by such labors you can achieve the most blessed happiness."

[Xenophon]: "This is roughly the way Prodicus pursues the theme of 'The Education of Heracles by Virtue.' Prodicus, however, adorned the ideas with even finer words than I have used just now."

Glossary

Abdera ('ab də rə)—ancient city in northeast Greece, near modern Turkey; home of Protagoras

Aeschylus ('es kə ləs) c. 525–456—one of the three great Athenian writers of tragedy

agonistic (ag ə 'nis tik)—relating to contest, struggle, or conflict of forces

agora ('ag ə rə)—market-place in ancient Greece where people met for social purposes, transacted business, and conducted civic affairs; like the Roman forum

antilogic (an ti 'lä jik)—an art or argumentative exercise originating in the fifth century which provided for examination of opposing sides of a proposition, e.g. of a certain measure as being just and unjust

apagogic method (ap ə 'gä jik)—a dynamic process of argumentation that provides for assessment of competing arguments and the

---

PRONUNCIATION GUIDE

ə	hunt, banana, about, militant		ī	life
a	back		ō	go
ā	take		ȯ	saw, log
ä	pot, tart		ȯi	coin
au̇	out		ü	truth
e	mess		u̇	foot, put
ē	eat, feet		yü	few
i	tip, radish			

71

ultimate rejecting of the unfavored; used by Gorgias in oratory

apology (ə 'päl ə jē)—a written or spoken justification of certain acts or alleged wrong-doing

archon ('är kän)—magistrate of the city; in the era of the great sophists, Athens had nine archons, each delegated specific duties

Areopagus (ar i 'äp ə gəs)—Athenian aristocratic council vested with supreme authority; as democracy came to Athens, the power of the Areopagus was limited to deliberating religious matters and trying murder cases

aretê (ar ə 'tā)—virtue and excellence and other qualities of citizenship

Aristophanes (ar ə 'stäf ə nēz) c. 450–c. 385—greatest of the Old Attic Comedy writers; Athenian whose plays are a key source of information on life in the fifth and early fourth centuries

Aristotle ('ar ə stät əl) 384–322—great Greek philosopher, born in the northern town of Stagira; pupil of Plato; tutor of Alexander (the Great); among his many works is the *Rhetoric*

Athenian Assembly (ə 'thē ni ən)—the *Ekklesia;* democratic assembly of male citizens over eighteen years of age that met to decide political questions, pass laws, and issue decrees

Athens ('ath ənz)—Greek city named for its patron goddess, Athena; artistic and cultural center of the Greek world in the fifth century

Attic Orators ('at ik)—ten Greek orators who lived in the fifth and fourth centuries and later, named as a standard of excellence; among them are Demosthenes (də 'mäs thə nēz), Lysias ('lis i əs), Aeschines ('es kə nēz), and Isocrates (ī 'säk rə tēz)

Ceos ('kē äs *or* 'sē äs)—island in the Aegean Sea, twenty-five miles off the mainland of southeastern Greece (Attica); home of Prodicus

Chalcedon ('kal sə dən)—ancient Greek colony situated across the Bosporus from modern Istanbul; home of Thrasymachus

Chalcidice (kal 'sid ə sē)—the triple peninsula in Macedonia (now part of northern Greece) that extends south into the Aegean Sea

Cicero ('sis ə rō)—106–43—great Roman statesman, orator, and author

Cleisthenes ('klīs thə nēz) of the late sixth century—statesman who as archon successfully promoted extensive democratic reforms; the founder of Athenian democracy

Cleon ('klē än) of the fifth century—Athenian politician and orator, usually portrayed as effective but vulgar and unscrupulous

Corax ('kor aks) of the fifth century—Sicilian Greek who, according to tradition, "invented" rhetoric at about 470 and taught Syracusans to argue in court when democracy replaced tyranny; he and/or Tisias reportedly wrote the first book on rhetoric, the first on any art

Cratylus ('krat ə ləs) of the fifth century—Greek philosopher, pupil of Heraclitus (her ə klī təs), and teacher of Plato; given the title role of Plato in one of the dialogues

Critias ('krit ē əs) of the fifth century—Athenian politician, poet, and one of the thirty tyrants; a character in Plato's dialogues

Crito ('krī tō)—friend of Socrates and a character in Plato's dialogues

Ctesippus (tə 'sip əs)—friend of Socrates and a character in Plato's dialogues

Delphi ('del fī *or* 'del fē)—Greek city high in the mountains eighty miles northwest of Athens, where the famous oracle resided; in ancient times, it was considered the center of the universe

dialectic (dī ə 'lek tik)—process of question and answer conducted according to certain rules and used to arrive at rational conclusions on chosen topics

dialogue ('dī ə lóg)—conversational discourse involving two or more people

Diodorus Siculus (dī ə 'dor əs 'sik yü ləs) of the first century—Greek historian who lived in Sicily

Diogenes Laertius (dī 'oj ə nēz lā 'ər shē əs) of the third century of the Christian era—widely cited Greek biographer

Dionysius of Halicarnassus (dī ə 'ni shi əs *of* hal i kär 'na səs) of the first century—Greek rhetorical scholar and historian

Elea ('ē lē ə)—city in southern Italy; place of the Eleatic school of philosophy with which Zeno was associated

Elis ('ē lis)—city in the Peloponnesus, near Olympia; birthplace of Hippias

encomium (en 'kō mē əm)—a formal expression of enthusiastic praise

Ephialtes (ef ē 'al tēz) of the fifth century—statesman who, with Pericles, was effective in passing measures that drastically reduced the power of the Areopagus and thus furthered democracy

epideictic (ep ə 'dīk tik)—relating to ceremonial or demonstration speeches of praise or blame

epideixis (ep ə 'dīks əs)—a public lecture or demonstration speech, e.g. one given by a sophist at a community gathering, panhellenic festival, or private meeting in a person's home

episteme (ep ə 'stē mē)—knowledge or body of knowledge

epistemology (i pis tə 'mäl ə jē)—study of the method and grounds of knowledge: how we come to know

eristic (i 'ris tik)—a form of disputation characterized by wrangling or specious reasoning

ethos ('ē thäs *or* 'e thōs)—one of the three classical modes of rhetorical proof: an appeal to the speaker's character, intelligence, or good will

Euripides (yù ′rip ə dēz) c. 485–c. 406—one of the three great Athenian writers of tragedy

Euthydemus (yù ′thid ə məs) of the fifth century—probably a contemporary of Socrates; given the title role in one of Plato's dialogues

forensic (fə ′ren sik)— type of discourse used in accusation or defense, e.g. in the courtroom

Glaucon (′glaü kὸn)—Plato's brother and a character in the *Republic*

Gorgias (′gor jəs) c. 484–c. 380—one of the five great sophists treated in this book

Helen (′hel ən)—the legendary and beautiful wife of Menelaus; her abduction to Troy led to the Trojan War; the woman whose face "launch'd a thousand ships" (Marlowe)

Heracles (′her ə klēz)—popular Greek mythical hero noted for his strength and courage; the subject of Prodicus's narrative on virtue vs. vice; Hercules

Hermes (′her mēz)—the winged messenger of the gods

Herodotus (hə ′räd ə təs) c. 484–c. 420—great Greek historian of the fifth century, known for his narrative of the war between the Greeks and Persians; the "father of history"

Hippias (′hip ē əs) c. 485 to 445–c. 390s—one of the five great sophists treated in this book

Hippocrates (hi ′päk rə tēz) c. 460–c. 370—recognized as the father of medicine; his writing was influenced by Gorgias, if not other sophists

Ionians (ī ′ōn i ənz)—philosophers of the sixth and fifth centuries, most of whom were from Ionia (present-day northwest Turkey) and who emphasized study of physical forces and composition of the physical universe

Isocrates (ī ′säk rə tēz) 436–338—famous Greek teacher of rhetoric and one of the Attic Orators

kairos (′kī räs *or* ′ker ōs)—the doctrine that guides a speaker on making good decisions in adapting to the nature of speaking situations and audiences

Leontini (lē ən ′tē nē)—ancient city of Sicily; home of Gorgias

logos (′lō gäs *or* ′lä gäs *or* ′lō gōs)—one of the three classical modes of rhetorical proof; appeal to reason

Lyceum (lī ′sē əm)—Athenian school established by Aristotle in 335: the "second university of the world" (Plato established the Academy fifty years earlier)

Lysis (′lī sis)—name of Plato's dialogue on friendship and one of the participants

Megara ('meg ə rə)—Greek city about twenty-five miles east of Athens; seat of the Megarian school of philosophy, one cultivating dialectical skills that eventually tended toward quibbling and eristic disputation

Menelaus (men ə 'lā əs)—legendary Greek king whose wife Helen—the most beautiful woman in the world—was carried off to Troy by Prince Paris, thus setting off the Trojan War

Meno ('mē nō)—dialogue of Plato in which Meno assumes the title role

metic ('met ik)—alien resident of an ancient Greek city

Olympia (ə 'lim pē ə)—plain in the northwest of the Peloponnesus

Olympic games (ə 'lim pik)—Panhellenic festival held every four years in Olympia, in the Peloponnesus, featuring contests in sports, music, speaking, and literature

paean ('pē ən)—a rhythmic pattern used in prose discourse, presumably discovered by Thrasymachus

Palamedes (pal ə 'mēd iz)—a hero of the legendary Trojan War but hated by Odysseus who cleverly arranged his death

pathos ('pā thäs *or* 'pā thós *or* 'pā thōs)—one of the three classical modes of rhetorical proof: emotional appeal

Peloponnesian War (pel ə pə 'nē zhən)—the long, disastrous struggle between Athens and Sparta which led to the downfall of imperial Athens—to the end of "the glory that was Greece" (Poe)

Peloponnesus (pel ə pə 'nē səs)—the large peninsula that constitutes the southwestern part of Greece; Corinth and Sparta were the principal ancient cities there

Pericles ('per ə klēz) c. 495–429—great Athenian leader of the fifth century who initiated extensive cultural development and democratic reform; died of the plague during the Peloponnesian War

Philostratus (fi 'lä strə təs) of the third century of the Christian era— author of *Lives of the Sophists*

Plato ('plā tō) 428–348—great Greek philosopher; pupil of Socrates and writer of dialogues, many of which reveal his criticism of democracy, indictment of the sophists, and view of rhetoric as representative of social imperfection

polymath ('päl i math)—a person of encyclopedic learning

Prodicus ('prä də kəs) c. 470 *or* 460- c. 390s—one of the five great sophists treated in this book

proem ('prō em)—an introduction, e.g. to a speech

Prometheus (prə 'mē thē əs)—the figure in Greek mythology who stole fire from the gods and gave it to humans; eventually punished by Zeus and in Aeschylus's account is chained to a rock and subjected to attacks by a great bird

Protagoras (pro 'tag ə rəs) c. 485–c. 425 *or* 415—one of the five great
   sophists treated in this book
Pythian games ('pi thē ən)—Panhellenic festival held every four years at
   Delphi (the third year of each Olympiad), featuring contests in
   sports, music, speaking, and literature
Socrates ('säk rə tēz) c. 470–399—great philosopher and mentor of
   Plato; principal character of Plato's dialogues
Solon ('sō lən) c. 639–c. 559—great Athenian archon, statesman,
   lawgiver, and poet who promoted political reforms that set the stage
   for greater democracy
sophist ('sä fəst)—professional teacher, e.g. of the fifth century as treated in this book
Sophocles ('säf ə klēz) c. 496–c. 406—one of the three great Athenian
   writers of tragedy
Syracuse ('sir ə kyüs, -kyüz)—city in Sicily and site of Greek colonies as
   early as the eighth century; visited several times by Plato
Theophrastus (thē ə 'fras təs) c. 371–c. 287—famous pupil of Aristotle
   and his successor at the Lyceum; rhetorical theorist
Thrasymachus (thrə 'sim ə kəs) flourished 430–400—one of the five
   great sophists treated in this book
Thucydides (thü 'sid ə dēz) c. 460–c. 400—great Greek historian of the
   Peloponnesian War; his writing was influenced by teachings of the
   sophists on rhetoric and human nature
Thurii ('thü rē ī)—a city of southern Italy on the Gulf of Tarantum
   (Taranto), near the site of old Sybaris
Timaeus (tī 'mē əs) probably of the fifth century—philosopher who was
   given the title role in one of Plato's dialogues
Tisias ('ti sē əs) of the fifth century—associated with Corax in develop-
   ing rhetorical theory in Sicily, c. 470; *see* Corax
Troy (troi)—ancient city near the Dardanelles (in modern Turkey) whose
   people fought the Greeks in the legendary Trojan War
xenophobia (zen ə 'fō bē ə)—fear or hatred of strangers or of things
   strange or foreign
Xenophon ('zen ə fən) c. 427–c. 355—Greek historian and observer;
   appreciative commentator on Socrates's life
Zeno ('zē nō) c. 490–c. 430—of Elea and the inventor of dialectic,
   according to Aristotle
Zeus (züs)—in Greek mythology, the king of the gods and men; husband
   of Hera

Works Cited and Other Useful Sources

WORKS CITED

Aristophanes. *The Clouds,* in *Aristophanes.* Trans. Benjamin Bickley Rogers. Cambridge: Harvard University Press, 1960.

Aristotle. *Rhetoric.* Trans. W. Rhys Roberts. New York: Modern Library / Random House, 1954.

Burnet, John. *Greek Philosophy: Part I, Thales to Plato.* London: Macmillan, 1914.

Bury, J. B. "The Age of Illumination." *The Cambridge Ancient History.* Cambridge: Cambridge University Press, 1958. 5:276-397.

Diodorus of Sicily. Trans. C. H. Oldfather. 12 vols. Cambridge: Harvard University Press, 1962.

Diogenes Laertius. *Lives of Eminent Philosophers.* Trans. R. D. Hicks. 2 vols. Cambridge: Harvard University Press, 1959.

Dionysius of Halicarnassus. *The Critical Essays.* Trans. Stephen Usher. Cambridge: Harvard University Press, 1974.

Durant, Will. *The Life of Greece.* Vol. 2 of *The Story of Civilization: Part II.* New York: Simon and Schuster, 1939.

Finley, M. I. *Politics in the Ancient World.* Cambridge: Cambridge University Press, 1983.

Gallop, David, trans. "Hippias." *The Older Sophists.* Ed. Rosamond Kent Sprague. Columbia: University of South Carolina Press, 1972.

Guthrie, W. K. C. *The Sophists.* Cambridge: Cambridge University Press, 1971.

Hadas, Moses. *The Basic Works of Cicero.* New York: Modern Library / Random House, 1951.

Havelock, Eric A. *The Liberal Temper in Greek Politics.* New Haven: Yale University Press, 1964.

Hegel, G. W. F. *The Lectures of Hegel on the History of Philosophy.* Trans. E. S. Haldane. 3 vols. London: Routledge & Kegan Paul, 1955. 1:352-384.

Jaeger, Werner. *Archaic Greece; the Mind of Athens.* Vol. 1 of *Paideia: The Ideals of Greek Culture.* Trans. Gilbert Highet. 2 vols. New York: Oxford University Press, 1945.

Kennedy, George. *The Art of Persuasion in Greece.* Princeton: Princeton University Press, 1963.

Kennedy, George, trans. "Gorgias." *The Older Sophists.* Ed. Rosamond Kent Sprague. Columbia: University of South Carolina Press, 1972.

Kerferd, G. B. *The Sophistic Movement.* Cambridge: Cambridge University Press, 1981.

Lamb, W. R. M. *Clio Enthroned: A Study of the Prose Form in Thucydides.* Cambridge: Cambridge University Press, 1914.

Plato. *Dialogues of Plato.* Trans. Benjamin Jowett. Chicago: Encyclopaedia Britannica, 1952.

Plato. *The Republic.* Trans. A. D. Lindsay. London: J. M. Dent and Sons, 1976.

Segal, Charles P. "Gorgias and the Psychology of the Logos." *Harvard Studies in Classical Philology.* Cambridge: Harvard University Press, 1962. 66:99-155.

Sparshott, Francis E., trans. "Thrasymachus." *The Older Sophists.* Ed. Rosamond Kent Sprague. Columbia: University of South Carolina Press, 1972.

Sprague, Rosamond Kent, ed. *The Older Sophists.* Columbia: University of South Carolina Press, 1972.

Untersteiner, Mario. *The Sophists.* Trans. Kathleen Freeman. Oxford: Basil Blackwell, 1954.

Usher, Stephen, trans. "On the Style of Demosthenes." *Dionysius of*

Halicarnassus: The Critical Essays. Cambridge: Harvard University Press, 1974.

Van Hook, La Rue, trans. "The Encomium on Helen, by Gorgias" (The Encomium of Helen). *The Classical Weekly* 6(1913): 122–123.

Vlastos, Gregory. Introduction. *Plato's Protagoras.* Ed. Vlastos. New York: Liberal Arts Press, 1956. vii–lvi.

Warrington, John. Introduction. *Plato, Symposium, and Other Dialogues.* Trans. Warrington. London: J. M. Dent and Sons, 1964. v–ix.

Xenophon. *Recollections of Socrates.* Trans. Anna S. Benjamin. New York: Macmillan, 1956.

OTHER USEFUL SOURCES

Adkins, Arthur W. H. *Merit and Responsibility: A Study in Greek Values.* Oxford: Clarendon Press, 1960.

Barker, Ernest. *Greek Political Theory: Plato and His Predecessors.* London: Methuen, 1960.

Beck, F. A. G. *Greek Education.* London: Methuen, 1964.

Dobson, J. F. *The Greek Orators.* Freeport, N.Y.: Books for Libraries Press, 1967.

Ehrenberg, Victor. *The People of Aristophanes: A Sociology of Old Attic Comedy.* New York: Schocken Books, 1962.

Gomperz, Theodor. *Greek Thinkers: A History of Ancient Philosophy.* Trans. Laurie Magnus. 4 vols. London: John Murray, 1955. 1:412–496.

Grote, George. "The Drama — Rhetoric and Dialectics — The Sophists." *A History of Greece.* 12 vols. London: John Murray, 1869. 8:118–204.

Harrison, E. L. "Was Gorgias a Sophist?" *Phoenix* 63 (1964): 183–192.

Havelock, Eric A. *Preface to Plato.* Cambridge: Harvard University Press, 1963.

Hinks, D. A. G. "Tisias and Corax and the Invention of Rhetoric." *Classical Quarterly* 34 (1940): 61–69.

Hudson-Williams, H. Ll. "Conventional Forms of Debate and the Melian Dialogue." *American Journal of Philology* 56 (1950): 156–169.

Hudson-Williams, H. Ll. "Greek Orators and Rhetoric." *Fifty Years (and Twelve) of Classical Scholarship*. Oxford: Basil Blackwell, 1968.

Hunt, Everett Lee. "Plato and Aristotle on Rhetoric and Rhetoricians." *Studies in Rhetoric and Public Speaking in Honor of James Albert Winans*. New York: Russell & Russell, 1962. 3–60.

Hussey, Edward. *The Presocratics*. New York: Charles Scribner's Sons, 1972.

Isocrates. "Against the Sophists." *Isocrates*. Trans. George Norlin. 3 vols. Cambridge: Harvard University Press, 1961. 2:160–177.

Jarrett, James L. Introduction. *The Educational Theories of the Sophists*. Ed. Jarrett. New York: Teachers College Press of Columbia University, 1969. 1–109.

Kerferd, G. B. "The First Greek Sophists." *Classical Review* 64 (1950): 8–10.

Kerferd, G. B., ed. *The Sophists and Their Legacy*. Wiesbaden: Franz Steiner Verlag GMBH, 1981.

Lewes, George Henry. *A Biographical History of Philosophy*. London: George Routledge, 1900.

Marrou, H. I. *A History of Education in Antiquity*. Trans. George Lamb. New York: New American Library, 1956.

Mill, J. S. *Dissertations and Discussions*. 2 vols. New York: Haskell House, 1973. 2:510–554.

Rankin, H. D. *Sophists, Socratics, and Cynics*. London: Croom Helm, 1983.

Robinson, Cyril Edward. *Hellas: A Short History of Ancient Greece*. Boston: Beacon Press, 1955.

Schiller, F. S. C. "From Plato to Protagoras." *Studies in Humanism*. 2nd ed. Westport: Greenwood Press, 1970.

Sidgwick, Henry. "The Sophists." *Lectures on the Philosophy of Kant and Other Philosophical Lectures and Essays*. London: Macmillan, 1905.

Sinclair, T. A. "Protagoras and the Others." *A History of Greek Political Thought*. London: Routledge & Kegan Paul. 43–68.

Smith, Bromley. "The Father of Debate: Protagoras of Abdera." *Quarterly Journal of Speech* 4 (1918): 196–215.

Smith, Bromley. "Gorgias: A Study of Oratorical Style." *Quarterly Journal of Speech* 7 (1921): 335–359.

Smith, Bromley. "Hippias and a Lost Canon of Rhetoric." *Quarterly Journal of Speech* 12 (1926): 129–145.

Smith, Bromley. "Prodicus of Ceos: Sire of Synonomy." *Quarterly Journal of Speech* 6 (1920): 51–68.

Smith, Bromley. "Thrasymachus: A Pioneer Rhetorician." *Quarterly Journal of Speech* 13 (1927): 278–291.

Smith, William A. *Ancient Education*. New York: Philosophical Library, 1955.

Versényi, Laszlo. *Socratic Humanism*. New Haven: Yale University Press, 1963.

Wilcox, Stanley. "The Scope of Early Rhetorical Instruction." *Harvard Studies in Classical Philology*. Cambridge: Harvard University Press, 1942. 53:121–155.

Zeller, Eduard. *Plato and the Older Academy*. Trans. Sarah Frances Alleyne. New York: Russell & Russell, 1962.

Notices of Copyright and Literary Property

Index